Its Raining Rent:

How to Make Money Purchasing and Renting Properties

From investment expert
Biff Sellers

Dunnmade books © 2019

Table of Contents

Its Raining Rent:

Find The Best Deals, Finance Smart, And Manage With Strength

Table of Contents

Introduction

Chapter 1: Property:
- Wealth For Today And Tomorrow
- The Safety In Rental Properties/ The Risks Of Real Estate
- The Buy And Hold Strategy

Chapter 2:
- The Best Towns For Rentals/ Best Neighborhoods
- Single or Multifamily Units
- Pets Or No Pets

Chapter 3:
- When Should I Buy?
- How To Finance And Pay For A Rental Property

Chapter 4:
- How To Repair And Maintain Rental Properties?
- Managing the Property

Chapter 5:
- How Do I Get To Dynasty Status?
- Commercial Real Estate

Chapter 6:
- What Properties Pack The Most Punch
- Training Your Tenants to Pay on Time
- Mistakes that Property Managers Make

Conclusion

Introduction

The following chapters will discuss why an income-generating property rental is a great way to make money, the basics of real estate rental investment, the different ways to make money in real estate investment, how to choose a profitable property rental and also what it takes to be a successful landlord. Commercial rentals may not be the common starting place for a beginner investor but this strategy is certainly worth a mention and worth pursuing once you've built up the capital and notched up a few years' valuable experience.

Real estate is just one of the types of many investment opportunities available. This long list includes foreign exchange speculation, savings accounts, and investing in stocks and bonds. These are among the more common. There is also, of course, the old method of stashing the cash under the bed. The last method guarantees no returns at all. The amount you put under the mattress is exactly what you take out from under the mattress. This works contrary to any investor's goal which is to make the most gains possible.

Ask anyone about the best ways to invest money and real estate investment will more often than not appear as the number one investment method. This is because investing in property is a tried and tested approach to building wealth more quickly than any other form of investment. Beginner investors face an exciting journey before them, especially if they decide to unleash their inner landlord.

No one likes to hear there are no shortcuts to success. But if you do hear it this should raise a very big red flag. Success, especially in real estate letting, is built on the back of planning, preparation and persistence. All three is required in formulating and implementing a business instrument every business person requires: the business plan.

Chapter 1:

Property

Wealth For Today And Tomorrow

Rental Property Investing is purchasing investment property for the purpose of renting it out for positive cash flow. It can be single family homes, multifamily units, apartment complexes or commercial property.

Rental property is using the property to receive a regular payment from those who choose to rent or lease. It is a great way to make a steady income. Unlike flipping where you fix and sell, you will receive smaller payments over an extended period of time.

There are several ways in which you can make money through rentals. If you buy and hold the property you can rent it out for the long term. This method will give you a consistently steady flow of income that could last you for years.

Another way you can make money on rental properties is to offer the home on a rent-to-own plan. This system is where the renter gives you a down payment and then pays you rent with the specific agreement that a percentage of the rent will be applied to the sale price of the home. At an agreed upon time, the renter can either return the property to you or pay it off based on the terms of the contract.

You are not limited to renting out apartments and homes. You can also rent out condos, townhouses, commercial property, and even land. With either option, you will receive a monthly income that can be applied to the mortgage, interest, and any maintenance needed to keep the property in livable condition.

One of the biggest advantages of rental property investing, is getting passive income. Having your property or investment work for you, and earn a income while you relax or move on to other projects. If done property, rental property investing can give you the freedom to live life on your terms and set your own schedule.

* You don't have to be present to make money. You can purchase a home and have the rest of the work subcontracted out, and earn positive cash flow.

* Rental property investing allows you to make money in a variety of ways. You can earn appreciation and on your property value and have your equity grow. You get tax benefits,

interest and business write offs for property ownership. You can get positive cash flow income from your tenant's rent.

* You have a variety of business models to choose from. Single Family, multifamily or commercial property.

* Real Estate Investing is one of the most sound and enduring businesses ever created. When I was a child, JC Penny's and Sears were the retail giants. They have been replaced by Amazon and Walmart. Real Estate investing will always be around because people will always need a place to stay.

* The principles for success are easy to understand. Buy at or below wholesale, rehab if necessary, rent or flip for a profit.

When you start a rental property business, begin with the end in mind. What strategy do you want to use? There are several types of strategies to decide on. For example:

* What type of property do you want to invest in? Single family, multifamily, commercial lease, apartments, condos or duplexes?

* How much money to you want to earn. Knowing that number will help you to decide what type of property you want to invest in.

* How will you finance your properties? High interest loans from private lenders? Deal with the regulations of traditional lenders or how about using credit cards?

* Where do you want to invest? Many suggest you start out, within one hour of where you live. But if you have really big financial goals, you may desire to invest nationwide.

* What is your time frame. "Dreams are goals with a deadline." Tony Robbins. You have to make a list of goals that are accompanied with deadlines.

* Are you going to manage your properties or hire a property management company?

* All business ventures involve risk. Expect the best, prepare for the worst. Business liability insurance will help, as well as the decisions you make involving financing and tenant selection.

* Vacancy. Eventually a tenant will move out. What model of marketing will you use to buffer the lost of a tenant.

* Passive income is not passive, if you are working on everything. How much are you going to delegate or subcontract out?

Once you select your overall rental property investment strategies you have to put a team together. You will need an attorney, accountant, real estate agent, repair man or maintenance person and a marketing person.

When you select an attorney make sure he or she specializes in real estate. They have to have a detailed knowledge of real estate contracts that are fair and protect you.

When it comes to accounting there are tons of software options out there that might persuade you to do your own accounting. You have to decide how much responsibility you want to have when it comes to accounting.

If you have a good real estate agent, they are well worth their commission. The best real estate agents work full time. They are more motivated because their dinner depends on their success. They should be able to give you accurate comps (Comparables is a real estate appraisal term referring to properties with that are similar, that have sold recently in the same area) and have a deep understanding of the real estate market.

Whether it's a single family, or much larger property, you should have a maintenance or repair person. Depending on the size of your business, you may need to have several maintenance personnel. If you decide to hire subcontractors, use references to make sure they are reliable.

Marketing. With the growth of the internet, there are now tons of ways to market your property. Your marketing can be as simple as business cards and a web site. Or your marketing could also be as detailed as creating YouTube videos for marketing in combination with other forms of social media like Facebook ads, email marketing, customer list building, article marketing and press releases.

Study to show yourself approved, a workman that need not be ashamed. Make educated decisions based on sound knowledge (people are destroyed for lack of knowledge). Learn from your mistakes.

Practice patience for your success. In the parable of the Chinese bamboo tree, speaker Les Brown teaches that the Chinese bamboo tree has to be watered every day while it grows for 5 years underground. Then it reaches enormous heights, shortly after it bursts threw the ground. Continue to water your breakthrough.

Make a decision to be determined to succeed. Set your goals. Make a plan. Then take action. Nothing worthwhile comes without challenges. Learn to enjoy the challenges, knowing that it is helping you to grow. After all, what's life without a little adventure.

The Safety In Rental Properties/ The Risks Of Real Estate

Investing in a rental property has its pros and cons. The positive sides of owning a rental property are many, and when investing wisely, the outcome can be a very lucrative one.

The Pros of Rental Investing

The benefit of owning a rental property is the income that is generated by what renters pay each month. If you have a property that your tenant pays $1,600 a month to rent, the income at year's end is $19,200. If you have financed the property, and are paying down a mortgage of $900 a month, and includes the property taxes, insurance, and interest, the annual income after expenses would be $8,400, $700 per month. If you paid cash for the investment, the total annual income after expenses is yours. Ideally, the location of the property has remained the same as when you first purchased the property. This will maintain the property's value. If the area has grown and new housing and shopping have moved into the neighborhood, this would be a good sign that the property value has appreciated as well.

Other financial benefits are repairs and renovations made to the property. Although it does cost to make repairs, upgrades or cosmetic changes to a property, the upside is that these repairs and renovations will increase its value. Pulling up an old carpet and installing hardwood flooring, installing impact windows, upgrading a kitchen or bathroom, even painting the property adds to its value. Added value can mean charging a higher rent and, if you decide to sell the property in the future, it can be sold at a higher value than when you first invested in the property.

When filing taxes, deductions can be declared on the property. Expenses incurred – mortgage interest, property taxes, operating expenses, depreciation, and any repairs are tax deductible. Expenses for managing the property, such as paying a property management company to manage it and doing the upkeep of the property by painting, or weatherproofing, as examples, can be tax deductible as well.

The financial benefits do not end with added value and higher rent when the property is upgraded, or tax deductions that can be taken at tax time. There are many other benefits that can be derived from owning a rental property.

Real estate prices do not vary on a daily basis as happens in the stock market. It is a relatively stable investment. However, the real estate market is not the same in all cities, so the ability to invest in property that can appreciate in market value can be more lucrative in some areas and not so much in others. Studying the community where you are having an interest in investing, is the best way to learn about whether your investment is going to produce a positive cash flow and, if you decide to sell, appreciate in value.

Real estate investing allows you to build a portfolio that will create a cash flow that can become your primary source of income. It gives you the freedom of setting your own schedule in maintaining the properties and control over how the properties are maintained.

As an investor, you can purchase properties that are below market value. Finding a property that may need a bit of work is worth the effort. If it is in a neighborhood that is attractive to renters, and where the market value of a renovated property will increase in value, then it is worth the investment.

Investment property will build equity. The rent collected will pay down a mortgage on the property and increase the equity. As you build equity, you gain leverage to purchase additional properties. More properties, more cash flow. You can save for a child's college education, build up a retirement fund, purchase a vacation home, or purchase more rental properties.

Another benefit when investing in rental real estate is the contribution to the community. Investing in a property that is a neighborhood eyesore and rehabilitating it improves the property for the neighborhood, subsidizes local taxes, and lifts up the appearance of the community. The residents are happy that a property in their area has a new face. Residents take pride in their community and a rundown property takes away the esteem of the area. Organizations can make contributions to a neighborhood for rehabilitating and improving schools, public parks, libraries, and the like, but improving a property and creating a home for someone is a great effort to provide for a community.

Investing in rental properties creates jobs. When a property is in the process of being rehabbed, local contractors, plumbers, roofers, electricians, and handymen are ready to offer their services and help create a livable space to rent.

Lastly, there is a benefit that is not always mentioned when investing in real estate. A rental property will provide a home for others. There are many people who do not have the funds to purchase a home, thus leaving them no other choice but to rent. Providing a beneficial and safe environment for a family, and living up to the responsibilities of a landlord is another to give to the community.

The benefits of investing in rental properties are many. If the investment is sound, it can provide a positive cash flow, build equity, create tax deductions, establish your presence in the community, and provide renters with a good place to live.

There is a downside to investing in rental properties that unfortunately can make investing in a rental property a not too pleasant experience, and could cost you more than you had anticipated.

The Cons of Rental Investing

The Disadvantage of not Diversifying

Investing in a rental property is that in owning a rental property, it ties up the finances of the investor and is not a liquid asset. This could be a potential problem.

The investor is locked into a property, on a particular block, in a specific neighborhood, in a specific city. If the neighborhood begins to decline, the investor loses a lot of money. If the block declines, more money is lost. If something happens to the house that the insurance can't handle, or it is not covered in the contract, the investor loses a lot of money. (Hamm, 2017)

When an investor needs to sell the property and the neighborhood has declined, the market value of the property will have diminished as well. It will not sell for as much as the investor had hoped when first purchasing it. It may take time to have the right buyer show interest in purchasing the property

The investor can sell the property even if there is a lease and a tenant. The new owner will purchase the property, honor the lease and allow it to run its term, and either renew the tenant's lease or put the property on the market for sale.

Real Estate Scams

A segment of Judge Judy gives an example of how an investment in a real estate transaction can go wrong. Unfortunately, the plaintiff had to take the defendant to court in order to get back his escrow deposit.

The plaintiff, we'll call him John, signed a contract to purchase an investment property from the defendant, named Bob. During the hearing, John gave Bob a $5,000 deposit to hold the property while he secured financing for the sale. John signed a contract but didn't ask questions about the terms. He just signed.

John thought the transaction was fine and proceeded to seek financing. However, the financing was taking longer than expected. One day, Bob called to ask what was going on with the financing. John still had not heard back from the lender and didn't have an answer for Bob.

A few days later, Bob calls John to say he had assigned the contract to another buyer, and that the other buyer would be purchasing the property. When John asked for his deposit back, Bob told him that he wasn't going to get it back because he "took too long" in financing the deal.

When the story was explained in court, Judge Judy said that the whole transaction sounded fishy to her. John was never told there would be a cutoff date on him securing financing. Bob never expressed that there was a cutoff, did not produce a contract that stated a cutoff, and felt that the property was off the market long enough. He wanted to make a sale, regardless of who purchased the property.

This incident is one of the negatives in investing in real estate. Jumping in just to secure a property without having the knowledge of how transactions work, signing a contract without asking questions about due dates for deposits, financing and closing the deal is a sure fire way of losing money even before you begin.

John won the case and Bob was ordered to return the $5,000. Not only had the possible loss of $5,000 being in jeopardy, but John had taken the time to file the complaint and wait until his case could be heard. An inconvenience and time wasted, not to mention the devious way Bob thought he could enrich himself with John's deposit.

Other types of scams that have been perpetrated against investors involve wire transferring funds to a title company whose account has been hacked. The deposit then gets deposited into a fraudulent account. The title company never receives the funds, and you're out the amount transferred.

Social media sites advertise unknown lenders, who promise to secure the funds for an investment transaction, take the escrow deposit and disappear.

Homeowners find out that their home has been used in a fraudulent property scheme. Their home is advertised as available for investment, when in fact, it is a privately owned home. Property owners, whose photos of their home and addresses are used to advertise and attract investors, are usually unaware of their homes being used in phony advertising schemes.

These are many of the kinds of real estate scams that can rob an investor in their investment finances. Needless to say, it's up to the investor to do their due diligence in checking out the validity of who they are dealing with, before signing a contract and turning over their deposit money. If you don't get the answers to questions about the contract, the property, and any contractual deadlines to be met from the seller, stay away. Legitimate real estate transactions happen when you work with reputable sellers, licensed real estate agents, and title companies, who are in the business to sell a property and achieve a positive outcome.

Repairs, Tenants and Maintenance

Owning a rental property can be time-consuming. Now that you've secured the property, does it need repairs, a major rehab, or just cosmetic fixes? You take on a risk and additional costs when you buy a property that needs repairs or upgrading. Dependent on the amount of work needed, and if you run into delays in getting the property up to code to make it a legal rental, you may find your finances negatively impacted, spending far more than budgeted.

When you own a rental property, you become a landlord. You have to deal with your tenants. You may want to hire a property management firm to be a buffer between you and the tenant, but you are still the landlord. Whatever the case, no decision about the property or the tenancy is made without your approval.

It would be a perfect world if tenants paid their rent on time. This can become a headache that will affect your cash flow if you have a habitually late or partial payer.

If they have pets, and even if they pay a pet deposit fee, there is still no guarantee that their pets will not destroy the property. One landlord could not believe that the bottom of one of her kitchen cabinets had been "eaten" by a tenant's dog.

Not everyone will treat your property as their own. This is a sad statement but true. The National Tenant Network or Rent Prep are two of the many companies that will do background checks of tenants for a fee. Using one of these firms to check on the background of a prospective tenant will give you a good idea of who you will be renting to. Contacting their former landlord as well can help keep negative situations from happening.

The maintenance of a property is very important in your role as a landlord. You are responsible for providing a habitable rental, suitable to live in, free of dangers or defects, and conforming to all state and municipal property and health codes. Providing heat, hot water, working plumbing, and a healthy environment is required as a landlord.

Investors should encourage that tenants have renter's insurance. The property is insured for anything catastrophic that can happen, but renters need to realize that their belongings are not covered by an investor's insurance on the property. There are very inexpensive, basic renter's insurance plans available. A renter needs to be proactive in protecting their belongings, especially if there are items that they need for their employment. PCs, laptops, musical instruments, work tools, anything that is kept within the four walls of a rental and belong to the tenant need to be covered by renter's insurance.

Any maintenance issues need to be addressed as immediately as possible. A leaking water heater that's over 15 years old needs to be replaced. An over the hill refrigerator that stops working needs to be replaced. When a roof that leaks after a heavy rain has leaked more than once, and finally leaks through a light fixture that could end up causing a fire, it's time for a new roof, not another patch job.

An air conditioning unit that is not working properly. The tenant calls to complain that it's 85 degrees inside while it's 95 degrees outside is a problem that needs to be fixed. The plumbing backs up and causes a flood inside the master bath, and master bedroom needs for a plumber ASAP. Unfortunately, it's Sunday and the plumber charges a premium to work on the weekend.

These are some of the problems that can occur when owning a rental property. Unfortunately, some of these problems come about because a landlord has been negligent in maintaining the property. A proactive approach to maintaining an investment property, will lessen the possibilities of major maintenance problems and expenditures, and keep the property in good rentable condition, thus providing the tenants a safe, hazard-free environment, and a continued cash flow.

For some investors, becoming a landlord takes too much of their time. If an investor is unable to meet the demands that are required or decides the hands-on role of maintaining their rental is not working for them, hiring a property management company would probably be a good way to have their investment managed. They can be a good landlord, yet free themselves of the day to day problems that may arise at the property.

One other downside to renting a property is evicting a tenant. If they haven't paid their rent and they are served with a 3-day notice to pay or vacate, or there are continued complaints from neighbors about loud, unnecessary noise that infringes on their peace and quiet, it's time to evict the tenant. Severe damage to the property by the tenants, their friends, other family members or their pets, and many other reasons a tenant could pose a hazard to the property or the neighbors is the time to file for an eviction.

There are negatives that can occur in investing in rental real estate. Knowing the pitfalls can help avoid them.

Investing in real estate rentals can be rewarding and profitable. It can create a supplemental income, positive cash flow, and tax deductions. The community you invest in benefits from attractive, rentable properties, and provide people with a clean, safe environment to live. By learning how to wisely invest, owning a rental property can be a great experience.

The Buy And Hold Strategy

Rental property is using the property to receive a regular payment from those who choose to rent or lease. It is a great way to make a steady income. Unlike flipping where you fix and sell, you will receive smaller payments over an extended period of time.

There are several ways in which you can make money through rentals. If you buy and hold the property you can rent it out for the long term. This method will give you a consistently steady flow of income that could last you for years.

Another way you can make money on rental properties is to offer the home on a rent-to-own plan. This system is where the renter gives you a down payment and then pays you rent with the specific agreement that a percentage of the rent will be applied to the sale price of the home. At an agreed upon time, the renter can either return the property to you or pay it off based on the terms of the contract.

You are not limited to renting out apartments and homes. You can also rent out condos, townhouses, commercial property, and even land. With either option, you will receive a monthly income that can be applied to the mortgage, interest, and any maintenance needed to keep the property in livable condition.

The many reasons why income-generating rental properties hold such high favor when it comes to a lucrative financial investment type include: being less of a risk factor (dependent on how long of an investment you have, above average returns on investment and you have relatively better management or control over your investment. Other ways income-generating property investment payoffs include:

1. Increase in asset value

Inflation can quickly decrease the buying power of your income. The increase in value and revenue from property rentals, on the other hand, offers outstanding asset appreciation value. This is due to rental increases and improvements and better management of real estate rentals.

2. Pride of property ownership

Among the many types of assets you can own, owning real estate generates the highest level of fulfillment. This is, however, dependent on finding the ideal location and ideal tenants.

3. Meaningful investment value

Real estate is a highly profitable investment choice. Defined as a hard asset, the grounds hold value, the structure or buildings hold value and the revenue received from rentals hold value. As property is a physical asset you can use this to leverage profit from more rental units or other investment types.

4. Favorable returns as compared to stocks and shares

Not only do you receive better returns than the stock market but real estate investment is not subject to constant change and upheaval influenced by external economic factors. For example, a natural disaster in Asia will not affect the value of the real estate you own on U.S. soil.

5. Your investment is protected

Owing stocks and shares offer little to no form of protection. If your investment in the stock market goes south, you could lose all of your shares portfolio value. With real estate investment, your land will always hold value and then theirs is the protective cover of home owners insurance.

6. Leverage from a diversified investment portfolio

Financial investment experts expound the many lucrative advantages of diversification. Through diversification, the risks are spread across many forms of investment

7. Tax advantages

Another hugely popular benefit of investing in real estate is the advantageous tax benefits offered to real estate investors. Some of the tax benefits include deductions on:

- home loan interest
- monetary gains from real estate rental properties
- related costs and management and maintenance expenses
- property taxes
- property insurance and depreciation

#7 Ways to turn a profit from renting out real estate

Investing in stocks offers only one avenue of receiving revenue and this is dependent on the stock's appreciation value and the opportune timing of selling the stock. There are more ways than one to turn a profit from income-generating real estate.

Here are a few to consider:

- Income generated from rentals.

This one needs no further explanation.

- Buy a property with a low market value

Buying low is a widely practiced method. You can make a quick profit from selling real estate for more than you paid for it. Properties with a low market price tag include foreclosure. Of course, this method is made even more profitable if you have the required negotiation skill set.

- Increase market value

Any improvements to the property increase its market value, allowing you to sell high. Unlike stock prices that are determined by the economic market, you have the choice of raising property value for higher returns.

- Improving equity

Every mortgage repayment you make towards your property rental increases equity value.

- Smaller property rental units can yield more returns than a larger single unit

By dividing one large sized house into different units you can rent these units out to a number of individual tenants and receive a larger sum in rent than just by renting out the house to one family.

- Rent out to businesses

The market places a higher price tag on property rentals to businesses. The best commercial client is an established business.

- Refinance property to improve cash flow

You can increase cash flow from property investment through refinancing. You can get more money into your pocket if refinancing allows for a decrease in mortgage repayments while the rental income you receive remain unchanged. The excess in cash flow received can be put towards the deposit for purchasing an additional property or saved for improvements or maintenance.

- Your success in income-generating property rentals depends on you

This is perhaps one of the best reasons to invest in property rentals as you are the critical factor in how well you do. You choose the area to purchase in, the type of property you want to rent out, the type of tenants you want to rent to (do you choose families or single professionals). Do you choose to buy a ready-to-move into property or a fixer upper as you're so handy when it comes to property D-I-Y? Do you manage and maintain the property yourself or do you outsource this to a property management company? How proactive are you in marketing your rental property and finding the best tenant?

- Even during economic turmoil, there are still advantages to owning rental property

Troubled economic times may not be all bad news for the property investor. There are potentially more people looking to rent having lost their homes to foreclosure and people being denied mortgage applications. And when the market stabilizes and improves, property prices will rise.

- As a tangible asset, property secures debt

If you've financed the purchase of property to generate income from it and for some reason you've defaulted on the repayments, you may lose the property and the income you receive from it but not your own house.

The more knowledge and research you acquire before delving into real estate investment, the fewer fears you may have about what the future holds.

Chapter 2:

The Best Towns For Rentals/ Best Neighborhoods

Rural Markets

If you are a future investor, you likely do not want to jump into the deep end of real estate investing by purchasing the most expensive condominium you can afford in downtown Manhattan, just to deal with a punishing mortgage for the next thirty years. It is in scenarios such as these that rural markets play an important role for the future mogul. Rural markets, as one would imagine, tend to be less expensive than downtown centers and urban markets. However, this is not always the case. It really depends in the type of rural market.

A hundred years ago, rich people owned properties in urban centers, such as New York and Chicago. The poor, on the other hand, lived in the outskirts of the cities or in rural areas. Currently however, the roles are changing. While many wealthy people still live in urban regions, we are experiencing a change in their patterns, as some very wealthy investors are purchasing rural properties. This is especially true for commercial farms, private ranches, and large estates, which may cost millions of dollars. While at first glance, the reader may be confused as to where to begin with rural markets, here is a neat trick: measure the distance of the rural markets to the nearest city.

Here's an example: let's suppose that Tyler lives in Baltimore and is looking to invest in rural properties near his home. Now for reference, Baltimore is 'happily' ensconced between two large urban areas – Washington, DC to the south, and Philadelphia in the north. Both of these cities, along with Baltimore itself, have their own suburbs, which take up a large portion of the surrounding areas. Therefore, if he is looking for cheaper properties, it is wise to not invest in such places in between Baltimore and Washington, DC. Rather, Tyler should look to the less populated eastern part of Maryland or across the Chesapeake to the west.

Assuming all other factors stay the same (ceteris paribus is the technical term in economics), similar properties to the east and west of Baltimore ought to be less expensive than those north or south of Baltimore, because they are closer to other urban areas.[8] That said, every neighborhood is different, so it's always necessary to do your homework in different regions before pouring your money into one property. The general statement does stand: rural properties are cheaper and therefore tend to require less capital to begin investing.

There are a two main advantages and disadvantages to rural properties being less expensive than urban properties. First, as previously hinted, because they are less expensive, the startup cash is not as prohibitive. A major hurdle to first-time investors is collecting the startup cash to purchase your first property. The less expensive rural properties are a major draw for first-timers. Well the simple math shows us how cheaper properties do not have much 'leverage' over more expensive ones. Because of this, property owners seeking to turn a profit from rural investments may have to be a bit lucky, or invest in many properties so that the passive appreciation of property adds to the investor's bottom line.

While there are clearly differences in price between rural and urban properties, there are other nuances that make rural properties a worthwhile investment. First is the difference in turnovers between rural and urban properties. The term turnover refers to the number of tenants that come in and out of your properties. Having a single renter in your property for fifteen years is a blessing in the real estate market. Dealing with changes in tenants at a bimonthly basis is painful and you will lose money with empty apartments along with the wear on your properties.

Because rural areas are less populated, there are fewer similar apartments or homes for people to move to, meaning that you are less likely to experience severe turnover in your investments. This stability is great for cash flow purposes, meaning that you will be less likely to be paying the mortgage on empty apartments.

For the same reason that there is little turnover in rural areas, there is also less competition from other investors, meaning that while the pond may be smaller, you're the bigger fish. This is especially true with older rural properties. Not only do they sell for less money, there is also less competition for them. Along this vein, there is an important point to be made. Because rural real estate is less competitive, it is not such a cutthroat industry as urban real estate, which resembles something closer to survival of the fittest. Especially when looking at rural properties, it is important to note that there are huge differences in the types of investments you can make. Barns, farms, and ranches all have different challenges, but one thing holds them all together: they are plentiful in rural areas. This solid supply of properties makes rural communities a viable place for the future mogul to invest their money.

Here's another advantage to rural properties: low taxes. Nothing absolutely destroys your bottom line as having to pay upwards of 60% of your tenants' rents in property taxes. Because rural communities tend to tax less (fewer schools, less infrastructure, etc.), back-end costs to investing in these regions may pay dividends in the long run. After all, taxes are a sunk cost – you cannot recuperate them and your benefits from them are indirect. Aligned with fewer property taxes, rural communities also tend to have less regulation. Since most people in rural communities are spread further apart than they are in urban sectors, it doesn't matter that much what they do in their own homes, leading to less overall regulation. Before we discuss suburban and town real estate markets, it's important to contrast the differences between rural and urban markets. In this spirit, this work will now look at urban markets so the reader can compare the differences with the rural markets.

Urban Markets

The first thing to know about urban markets is that they are all extremely different. Just like in the game Monopoly, the differences between Mediterranean Avenue costing $60 and Boardwalk setting you back $400 are staggering. Unlike rural markets where an investor can clearly notice the differences between an expensive ranch and a run-down barn, these distinctions are blurred in urban markets. On top of this, each city in the United States has a slum and skyscrapers with million-dollar penthouses. The staggering differences between properties in urban markets can leave potential investors lost, so here are some details that may smooth out the transition for the reader.

The first thing the reader should know about urban markets is that prices vary greatly from neighborhood to neighborhood in urban markets. San Francisco and New York are the two most obvious examples of overpriced housing cities in the United States. Take a look at the chart below illustrating the disparity in home values in San Francisco as compared to other cities in California.

Figure 2: Home Prices in California (Source: Winzer 2018)[9]

This chart tells us a lot about the disparity of home prices in one single state. First let's take a look at the notoriously expensive San Francisco. Judging from the average home price column, we see that San Francisco is the only city in California with an average home price of just over a million dollars.

This means that if the investor would like to purchase a property there, they would need substantially more capital ($200,000 for a 20% down payment) than if they were to purchase a property in Bakersfield, with an average property value of $189,000. The down payment for the average home in this city is $37,800, a fraction of the down payment for the average home in San Francisco. Now some readers may be looking at San Francisco with a jaundiced eye, so here is some more information on expensive urban markets that may sway your mind.

First, the reader must always keep in mind that there is a reason why San Francisco is expensive. It's an ideal place to live. The weather is great year round, tenants are close to both the ocean and mountains, high-tech jobs are plentiful and nearby, and the city has a vibrant culture that attracts Millennials and empty nesters[10] alike. Due to the combination of these factors, San Francisco enjoys not only high property values, but also better properties. This ultimately would increase the average price of properties in the city, hence the million-dollar row homes and brownstones. As is often stated in real estate, location is the best predictor of success.

Next, not all of us have $200,000 lying around to invest in one property. This leads us to point out the second nuance when looking at the San Francisco market: you don't have to buy the most expensive property, or even the average-priced property. Just because the average price of a home in San Francisco is over a million dollars doesn't mean that there aren't cheaper alternatives.   When analyzing real estate markets in expensive cities, such as Los Angeles or New York, make sure to determine price differences between various neighborhoods. This is another advantage urban markets have over rural ones. The investor can differentiate between property prices in the same neighborhood. This type of homogeneity is unlikely to be found in rural communities, where similar cookie cutter properties do not exist. Along this vein, it is also a good idea to scrutinize how these properties have changed in price over time.

Let's take a second look at the urban markets in California. Naturally, we see San Francisco, Anaheim, Oakland, and Los Angeles as enjoying (or suffering from) expensive housing markets, but what about the changes in price of these markets? Every city in California is experiencing an increasing in housing value over time, as we don't see any negative numbers in the 'Home Price Change' column above. However, some markets are increasing at a faster rate than others. It sure looks like San Francisco is plateauing at a 6% increase in home values, though this is still pretty good. Yet, take a look at Fresno, Yuba City, Merced, Hanford, Sacramento, and Stockton. All of these cities are experiencing growth at double-digit rates, with Yuba City reaching a 13% change in home price. For the real estate investor thinking of investing in urban markets, these properties offer the highest ROI in terms of passive appreciation. But how does the future investor know what to expect in terms of rent for their urban properties?

As the reader will recall from the previous section, there are two primary ways to make money in the real estate market: rent from tenants and property appreciation. If the investor is looking for property appreciation, they will do well to look at the red column in Figure 2 denoting 'Home Price Changes.' Yet, how can the investor know what to charge for rent? Simple, use the 1% rent rule. This rule states that the average value a property can be rented out for is 1% of the total cost of the property.

So, let's imagine that Matt holds a property in Modesto, CA that costs around $250,000, which is about average for that city. Since Matt is a profit-maximizer, he is looking to rent out his property for the most amount of money. However, if the price is too high, then nobody will rent out Matt's property and he will have to lower his price. This creates a balance—a sweet spot of sorts—between the prices that a renter is willing to pay versus the price an investor wishes to charge. If Matt is familiar with the 1% rent rule, then he can find this balance quite easily. He simply takes 1% of $250,000, which is $2,500 and charges that figure for rent. If Matt's property is a condo with multiple bedrooms and bathrooms, then he has the opportunity to split that rent between two or three tenants.

There is another advantage to investing in urban properties over rural ones. Urban properties are remarkably easy to resell. Because of the lower level competition in rural markets, there are fewer people vying for fewer properties, rendering such markets more difficult if the investor is looking for a fixer-upper or to turn properties quickly. Fixer-uppers, as the name suggests, are those often-foreclosed properties that an investor buys at a discount from a bank, fixes them up, and then resells them for a profit.

This style of real estate investing works much better in urban markets that in rural markets precisely because of the fast resale rates of urban markets. Put in economic terms, urban markets are more 'liquid,' meaning that they can be turned into cash on hand, than rural markets.

But for now, it's important for the future mogul to know that this is a way to invest in the urban real estate market, if done correctly, for some serious profits.

Yet another advantage to the urban market is property appreciation. As hinted by the figure in the previous pages, urban markets in California are all appreciating in value, yet at different paces. Some, like San Francisco, seem to be plateauing while others, such as Fresno, are booming. As a general rule of thumb, the investor should be wary of small percentages of appreciation in value in smaller cities. Investing in a shrinking economy is generally not a good idea, especially if this economy correlates with a shrinking population. Rural markets move on a much slower time scale, thereby appreciating at far gentler a rate than urban markets.

Suburban Markets

When investors talk about different real estate markets, they tend to simply differentiate between rural and urban regions, assuming that suburbs are simply the halfway point to both markets. This could not be further from the truth. Suburbs may as well be their own animal when it comes to real estate investing, so this section is dedicated to showing you how to differentiate between suburban properties and where the pros and cons are for this market. First and foremost, as an investor, the last situation you want is empty rooms with a mortgage. These scenarios force the investor to continue paying for the home, along with taxes and insurance, without tenants actually using the homes themselves and paying rent.

With this knowledge in mind, a unique and positive characteristic of the suburban real estate market is the slow turnover rate. The reader will recall that turnover is the changing of tenants over and over again. As an investor, this unreliability in renters creates more paperwork, leaves more to chance, leaves apartments empty, and leads to less stability.

All of these factors increase uncertainty and lead to less confidence in investing. Luckily, suburban markets are reliably stable. Tenants choosing to live in suburban markets tend to have small families, have stable jobs, can pay rent, and tend to save money. Because of this, they often prefer more permanent locations. When investing in suburban real estate markets, pay special attention to the school districts there, as many parents with young children will move to better school districts so that their children can have a better education than they would have elsewhere. If your property can attract these tenants, you will likely have renters in these properties for a long time.

The downside to these more permanent tenants is that there may be a lack of interest in renting. Most people who live in suburbs are small families or those looking to have a family of their own in the future. This means that there may be an overall interest buying homes rather than renting them for long periods of time. However, as previously stated, if they have small kids, they may interested in changing homes due to more competitive school districts in some neighborhoods over others. Where the future investor can distinguish herself is in knowing their clients and their needs. The real issue here is that those who live in suburbs are accustomed to 'owning' their possessions. They likely have their cars paid off, have their own furniture, and are generally more interested in owning a home as well. Connected to owning a vehicle, there is additionally a general lack of public transportation in suburban parts of the United States. While it is nearly impossible to move in urban areas without public transportation, very few buses and subways reach suburban communities.

Connected to the permanence of the tenants in suburban markets is that they tend to treat your properties with greater care. Because of this, the appliances of the home tend to be taken care of at a better rate than in urban sectors where tenants may move from property to property with little care for the appliances. Since many children are living in these suburban properties, parents usually wish to teach them good cleaning and maintenance habits, leading these units to be a better 'bang for your buck' as an investor. This respect for your property goes a long way in its resale value, especially if your tenants view your property as a home, rather than as a temporary living space.

Another unique characteristic of suburban real estate is the sheer difference in size per square foot of property. Let's suppose that Sean is looking to either invest in Tulsa city proper, or one of its surrounding suburbs. If he is looking for a $200,000 property, he can likely get a unit with 2000 square feet in Tulsa, or 6000 square feet of property in one of its suburbs. This three-fold increase in suburban property sizes makes the investor 'feel' as if they have more property, and ultimately equates to more physical property than investing in urban sectors. Combined with this extra space is a backyard. Many tenants hoping to have a quieter life in the suburbs enjoy properties with some space. It then follows logically that if you are thinking of investing in the suburbs, the properties you look for should have at least a small backyard or a large-enough front yard.

There are two more, intertwined, aspects of investing in suburban properties. First, suburbs have a huge decrease in crime rate as compared to urban centers. This naturally renders them more appealing to families looking for safety for their children. Along this track, suburbs tend to also be quieter than urban areas, though, of course, not as quiet as rural properties. Many suburbs also offer enough evening activities to keep adults busy without overloading them with the constant neon glow of city lights. Suburbs are usually home to high school football stadiums, guilds, societal clubs, and the like that provide enough entertainment for tenants without forcing them into overdrive. Suburbs are also much more spread out than urban areas, but since many homes are similar, purchasing various single-property homes in one suburb is a viable investment option for the future real estate investor.

The final characteristic of suburbs is the location. They are far away enough from cities that these properties are not as loud, but not in rural parts of the United States that lack amenities. Suburbs offer easy-enough access to city life should tenants choose to go into the city, while offering the accommodations of more space and tranquility in rural regions. As with any suburb, there are dozens of different neighborhoods that offer a variety of income levels and properties for investment. Real estate investment strategies may change from neighborhood to neighborhood, contingent upon school districts, crime, and noise levels by restaurants and bars.

Now that the reader has a decent idea of how to make money as a real estate investor and knows how to differentiate between urban, rural, and suburban markets, it is now time to discuss the differences between tenants. There are two primary types of investments: single-family real estate investment and multi-family real estate investment. Let's take a look below at the two different types of investments and how they differ.

This section of the guide will look at some of the most vital things to consider when searching for the right property. Your analysis should be thorough. Replace your sentiment with intense analyzing and you will do fine (the next section will cover smart calculations you need to do when looking for the perfect property).

Here are the things you should consider:

1: The Neighborhood

The type and quality of neighborhood you choose will influence the kind of tenants you attract as well as how often you deal with vacancies. Take the example of a neighborhood located near a university. Such a rental property will attract university students. While your prices may have to be relatively low to accommodate students, you will most likely have a healthy traffic of renters. However, you can also expect occasional vacancies such as during holidays when students tend to home.

2: The Property Taxes

The previous section mentions taxes, and the unique tax-cap rental properties attract. You also need to understand that property taxes are not usually standard across the board.

As a property investor looking to earn a passive income from rent money, you will want to know how much you are losing to the taxman. The truth is that high property taxes may not necessarily be a bad thing if you own property in an excellent neighborhood with a minimal rate of vacancies. The trouble is that these two do not always go hand in hand. Your town's assessment office (there is one for sure) will have all the necessary tax information on file. If this is too much work, you can always talk to the homeowners in your community.

3: Schools

If you are targeting couples as the ideal tenants, you can bet that children may be on the agenda and that they will be looking for property with a nearby school. When you find good property near a school, your first step should be to find out the reputation and quality of the school.

What does a school have to do with your property? Well, the quality of the school will directly influence the value of your property. If the school's reputation is poor, your investment will also be poor in value, which will make it hard to justify your prices even if they are reasonable. Even if this is not the case, if you do decide to sell your property at some time, your projected value and the projected value of your potential buyers will be dissimilar.

4: Crime Levels

Few people will fancy living next door to a crime hotspot. Even testosterone junkies prefer their roughhousing served at the confines of bars. Take your time and visit the public library or the police station for accurate stats on crime rates. Asking the man/woman selling you the property about it is lazy and ill informed. Why would he/she jeopardize the sale by telling you anything other than what you would want to hear?

Here are some things to check: serious crimes, rates of vandalism, petty crimes, and the most recent crime activity (slow down or growth). You may also consider asking police frequency in the neighborhood.

5: The Job Market

Locations that boast growing employment opportunities will tend to attract more people and more tenants. There is a way to find out how a neighborhood rates on this one. Go straight to the U.S Bureau of Labor Statistics or the local library.

If you hear of a new company moving into the area, your smart money will be on potential workers flooding in. Sure enough, this will negatively or positively reflect on the house prices. The former is most likely. Nevertheless, here is your fallback: as a smart investor, figuratively speaking, you will want the new corporation to be in your backyard.

6: Amenities

Check your potential neighborhood for current parks or any projected ones. Check for malls, gyms, public transport hubs, movie theatres, and other amenities that will attract tenants. Most cities will have promotional literature that gives you an idea of where the ideal blend of amenities and private property merge.

7: Building Permits and Future Development

The municipal planning department will usually have all the information you need on new developments coming into your area of interest. If you notice new condominiums, malls, and business parks cropping up in the area, it is a sign that the area is a good growth area.

However, before jumping in feet first, it will be smart to look out for any new developments, which could actually end up hurting your investment or the surrounding property pricing. For instance, is there a new development that will, in the end, cause the loss of friendly green space?

What about those additional condominiums coming up; will they offer intense competition for your renters? The idea here is to target an area that shows signs of healthy growth but at the same time, determine if the healthy growth is healthy for your investment.

8: The Number of Listings and Vacancies

Take this one very seriously. If the prices of the properties are unbelievably good, but when you look into it, the neighborhood shows an unusually high number of listings, perhaps this may be due to a seasonal cycle, in which case, you should not shirk from making your purchase.

However, it could also be a sign that the neighborhood has gone bad. Before you invest, determine which one it is. You should also determine your ability to cover any season-based fluctuations related to vacancies. Similar to listings, vacancies rates will give you a clear picture of how successful you are likely to be at attracting new tenants and retaining them. Here is some basic math for you: high rates of vacancies FORCE proprietors to lower rent rates in a bid to attract tenants. Low rates of vacancies ALLOW property owners to raise rent rates.

Single or Multifamily Units

Most people would prefer the multifamily units because they feel that these will generate a lot more income than a single-family unit. With a multifamily unit you have the potential for greater income, however, you also have a lot more work involved. If you plan on managing the property yourself and not hiring a management company to do it for you, then maybe single-family units would be a better option.

If you have the time to dedicate to the property, and the resources to keep a maintenance crew on hand, then a multifamily unit may work. You have to take the time to evaluate your personal circumstances to decide which option will suit your life and goals best. While you may have big dreams with lots of dollar signs in your eyes, it is very important for you to be honest with your personal appraisal of yourself. The best investment option for you will depend on what you are capable of handling, how much commitment you have, and what you realistically can expect to gain.

It is not enough to find a single-family unit at market value. If you really hope to turn a profit in this industry, start from the beginning looking for those properties that are selling below market value. It is the main reason you'll get excellent returns on your rentals. Some real estate experts will only look at properties that are selling at 70-80% below market value. These are usually fixer-uppers and have been that way for an extended period of time.

When you can find property below market value, you make money in two ways. First, your property value goes up as soon as you close because you bought below market, but you will also add value from the improvements you make. Add to that, the rental income if you decide to lease the units and you have a pretty easy steady income in your future.

Pets Or No Pets

The decision to rent to pet owners is a personal one. It also depends on the kind of pet. If they have a dog that loves to chew on furniture or has a very destructive nature then you will rightly be very concerned about renting to them. However, if they have a pet that is calm, friendly and won't be a threat to the neighbors, then you can make room for him in your place.

You can require an additional deposit for pets in case of damage. Pets can easily destroy carpeting, flooring, and even drywall. Some have been known to chew on doors or dig up and destroy beautifully manicured lawns.

True pet lovers won't hesitate to pay an additional deposit for their pets to have a home. They may even be willing to pay more in monthly rent just to keep their loved one with them. This can definitely make it worth your while, on the long run, to have a pet stay in your place. As a general rule, consider gauging the extra charge based on the size of the animal. The larger the animal the more damage he could do, therefore the more the tenant should have to pay.

You also need to check with your local city ordinance about the kinds of pets allowed in the community. You may be okay with a pit bull on your property, but some city ordinances have strict regulations against such breeds. If something were to happen, then you would be held liable for allowing the pet on your premises.

Some pet owners will state that their pet is a little angel. How can you know for sure? One of the best ways to find out is to talk to previous landlords to find out what the pet was like in the last home. You can also request them to bring the pet in so you can see how he interacts with others.

It pays to put a clause in their lease that stipulates that if they do not comply with your regulations on pets on the premises they can be fined an additional fee for the inconvenience.

How can we avoid a situation like the one above? That is a tricky question, because a landlord can do all the right things and still end up as the responsible party. That's why I always like to manage the what if. For example, at our multi-unit buildings, we just don't allow pets. With a multi-unit building, tenants live very closely together with no yard, therefore I think it is risky to allow tenants to have pets.

For our single-family rentals, we do allow pets, but under one condition. The tenant must have renters or liability insurance that includes pet insurance. We also require the tenant to put us (the landlords) and the property management company on the tenant's policy as "additional interest," so if the tenant stops paying their premiums, the insurance company will notify us. I also make sure it is stated in the Rental/Lease Agreement that the tenant must continue to have active renters/liability insurance that includes a pet policy.

Chapter 3:
When Should I Buy?

Now, that you've got all your ducks in a row, it's time to go shopping. You know about the different benefits of real estate and you're ready to take the plunge. You have established a good relationship with your bank and you've got your financing at least in the preliminary stages. All you need to do now is find your first piece of property. But where should you look?

Finding Property

If you've been a renter up until now, you already know that there is more than one way to find a rental. But things can be a little different when you're looking for a place to buy. You obviously won't be looking in the same places for properties to buy, but there can be some overlapping. However, with real estate, there are some places that a renter would never go to find a place to live. Let's take a look at these places first.

Real Estate Auctions

There are many places where real estate is auctioned off. Most of the properties sold at auction are foreclosures. You can find some of the lowest prices at these sites. There are live auctions and online auctions so depending on the type of property you're interested in, you'll have to participate with either one of them.

One of the first places to look is online or in your local newspaper. Before you engage in an auction, you first need to learn the rules of the auction site. If you're looking in a newspaper, there should be some type of legal notice of any upcoming auctions. Make a note of the auction companies so you can visit their website directly to find out about what their requirements are to enter.

Government Websites

Foreclosed properties can also be found on several government websites. They maintain a listing of upcoming auctions for properties that have outstanding taxes due. These are properties that weren't foreclosed on because of not paying their mortgage but from not paying their taxes. You can find some pretty affordable properties here for a song.

Fannie Mae will first try to sell their own foreclosed properties before they put them up for auction. However, if for some reason they are unable to sell it the traditional way, they will put it up for auction through HomePath.com.

You can also check the U.S. Department of Agriculture and the Federal Deposit Insurance Corporation for properties they may be planning to auction.

The U.S. Treasury: https://www.treasury.gov/auctions/treasury/rp/.

Fannie Mae foreclosures through Home Path: https://www.homepath.com/investors.html

Your Bank

Some banks have an inventory of properties on their website. These lists can be found by doing a Google search with the name of the bank and the term "REO" which means Real Estate Owned or bank-owned.

Zillow.com

This has a list of properties for sale. Their filtering option allows you to narrow down your search to only include foreclosed or rehabbed properties

Real Estate Broker

You can never go wrong by asking a real estate broker for possible auctions in your area.

Find Absentee Owners

Another, more creative way to find property is to approach an absentee owner of the property and make a private deal. With a competitive market like real estate, sometimes listed properties are receiving multiple offers that you may have little or no chance of getting into. Sometimes your best shot is to get to a property before it is listed.

An absentee owner is an individual who owns a property but lives elsewhere. They may be a landlord or they may have inherited the property from someone. This approach may take a bit of work, but it can certainly pay off in the end. You can find these properties by:

- Driving around a neighborhood looking for vacant homes
- Online public records can help you find the owner
- Buy a public record listing from a source like ListSource.com

- Calling owners of places for rent

When it comes down to it, finding the right property to buy is a numbers game. The more properties you look at, the better your chances of finding something that will pay off in the end.

Choosing the Right Property

Once you have your listings, you should collect several properties to look at, so you can evaluate and compare. The priority now is determining which property will be a good investment. Reaching a conclusion will not always be easy due to the numerous factors for you to consider.

You will need to know exactly what you plan to do with the property. If you're purchasing rental properties, there are different factors to consider as opposed to purchasing property to flip or rehab.

For Rental Property

Your strategy here should be about finding something that you can be comfortable with. When looking at property, avoid thinking only about the risk. While that is important, there are many other things to consider when deciding on a rental property. Many new investors start off by expecting to find a perfect unit straight out of the gate, but this is rarely the case. You can expect, even in a well-structured building that you're going to have to do some work to get it up to speed.

In addition to getting the property below market value, with these types of properties you also have to factor in the cost of maintenance, managing the property, and cost of repairs, vacancies and a host of other things. To help you to decide if the property is right for you, here are a few basic guidelines.

- Single-Family Residence: These are considered the best option for a new investor. If you already own a home then you already have a good idea of the costs to keep it maintained for a renter. This information makes the initial evaluation of the property relatively easy. You also need to factor in the cost of water and sewer hook-up if it hasn't already been included. The only decision you have to make beyond the estimate of costs is whether you want long-term renters or vacation renters.

There are several advantages to this type of rental property. First of all, you only have to deal with one responsible party for the rent, so it is easy to keep records. You can include the cost of utilities in the rent or have your tenant accept responsibility for these additional expenses. And it is only one structure, so you do not have a lot of buildings that need to be maintained. If you don't have a lot of time to manage a property, then this type of investment may be your best option.

However, even in single-family dwellings, you are likely to be responsible for maintaining the exterior, which includes the lawn and landscaping. If you were to purchase a condo or a town home, then you would be paying HOA fees that will also have to be factored into the overall costs. Make sure you budget for vacancy periods. With only one unit as your income, vacancies can hit your pocketbook pretty hard.

- Duplex/Triplex: These multifamily units can make a huge difference financially when compared to a single-family dwelling. You can live in one unit and rent out the others saving you on expenses. Make sure that you can collect enough rent to cover both the unit you are living in and the one you're renting out. If you choose a triplex, you also have a little cushion in case of a vacancy.

Depending on the location, these can work great in university towns or areas where many singles tend to live. The expenses are easily managed, and you still only have one building to maintain.

Still, you will have additional expenses to contend with. You will be responsible for several meters for utility services or have to create a way to manage these expenses so that they are fair for all concerned.

- Apartments: Purchasing an apartment building may not be as easy an investment to get into as the other options. These can easily run up into the millions of dollars and getting enough credit to cover the cost can be quite difficult. However, if you have an apartment building in your sites it may be best to approach the project with a partner or a group to help you foot the bill. If you can, there are plenty of benefits that make good reasons to pursue apartment rentals.

As a first time investor, consider starting out with a smaller apartment building with four to ten units. These are much easier to get into for an individual investor, but you will have a lot more risks associated with it. If you go in with a partner you will have a lower risk and you have more protection from vacancies. If one unit is empty, there is still enough wiggle room to make a clean profit.

On the other hand, if you have multiple units empty you can incur severe losses, especially if the condition continues for an extended period of time. Factor in additional maintenance expenses and consider having tenants responsible for their own utilities to make it easier.

- Condos: Condos, like apartments, can be rented out. These actually make for great vacation rentals but expect to pay additional HOA fees in addition to other expenses. If this is your plan, make sure vacation rentals are allowed in the building. Some HOAs do not permit them so you want to check this out before you buy.

Keep in mind, that the HOA has the final say as to what kind of upgrades and changes you can make on the property. You may be restricted as to installing internet, satellites, or even what colors you are allowed to paint. There is also the issue of the neighbors, which could also restrict you on what liberties you can take with your unit as to rental property.

- Commercial Property: If you are interested in purchasing a commercial property keep in mind that your tenants will be businesses. On the surface, these can appear to be very lucrative opportunities, but it is best that you proceed cautiously. In recent years, we have seen many brick and mortar businesses fail because of competition from online stores, which offer a lot more convenience. When evaluating these types of properties, you need to think in an even wider scope. Learn the fundamentals of the business as well as their ability to turn a profit. Think about their competition, not just locally but online as well, their reputation in the community, and their product or service. All of these will have a bearing on your bottom line when they rent from you.

The good news is that business tenants tend to pay more in rent than a residential tenant. If you acquire an entire building, you can have the benefit of multiple tenants paying rent, thus increasing the amount of revenue you can generate.

You will have additional expenses to factor in. By law, you will have to maintain a commercial property-liability insurance plan, which can be quite costly. There will be a high initial outlay of cash to buy the property, which may mean that you will have to take on a partner or a group of partners to fund the project. Maintenance expenses will be higher and there is still the expenses of vacancy periods, which are often more difficult to fill in commercial property.

When trying to decide which type of investment property is right for you, your number one concern is expenses. Unlike when you are dealing with an individual purchase for personal use, there are many factors that need to be weighed in order to find the right property. At the very least, factor in all expenses, add in another 10-20% for those unexpected ones and then weigh those against the potential income the property will generate.

This is much harder if you're looking at flipping houses or rehabs. There are, of course, those obvious costs, but often in such buildings, additional surprises come up that could easily curtail your project. By taking all of those into consideration, evaluating how much time and money you have to invest, you can narrow down your options and find the right property to invest in.

About Vacation Rentals

It is estimated that the vacation rental industry is expected to generate $36.6 billion for the coming year. This figure is partly due to the fact that travelers have discovered that they can pay the same amount of money as an expensive hotel and get a more home-like experience with additional space and amenities to boot.

Vacation rentals can be a highly lucrative investment option but there are a few things you need to keep in mind before you decide to jump in and try your hand at this business.

- Vacation homes are just like any other hospitality business. You will take on a long-term responsibility, so you need to have your objectives clearly in mind.

- The location should be of primary importance. Finding a great deal in an area where tourists do not frequent won't get you very many guests to occupy your home. Look for properties in well-established areas where you can reasonably expect tourists will want to visit.

- Quality is paramount. Your guests will be paying prices comparable to a high-quality hotel, so they will expect accommodations that will be better than a standard home to live in. It doesn't need to be in a resort, but you will have to offer them something that will be a cut above the average living conditions they would normally receive at home.

- Mixed developments do not work well for vacation rentals. Vacationers are more comfortable with other vacationers, and full-time residents will feel more at ease if their neighbors are not changing every week.

- If you can hire a management company it can make a huge difference in vetting the guests before they come to rent your place. Because the turn-over of occupancy changes frequently, they can handle all the little details that will ensure that your guests get the best experience possible. They can verify that payments are made and that the guests have something special that they will remember and talk about when they return home.

If you want to be a part of a growing industry, vacation rentals can generate far more cash flow per year than the average home rental. However, you will have to raise your standards considerably in order to attract the kind of clientele that will be willing to pay the premium prices that these kinds of rentals demand.

The Short Sale

When looking for that perfect deal on a piece of property, there are many roads you can take. Ideally, you are looking to find the property at the best price possible and one way to get a significant break in the expenses is through a short sale.

A short sale is when the homeowner agrees to sell his property for less than what is owed on the mortgage. You might wonder why a property owner would consider making such a deal. If he sells short, he could still be on the hook for the remaining balance on the mortgage.

While short sales are not as common as they once were, they are a great way to help homeowners who are underwater or behind in their mortgage payments. In other words, they find that they owe more on their homes than it is actually worth.

You can find short sale listings in the same place as you would find other property listings. Their posting will specifically say 'short sale or subject lender' so that potential buyers will know exactly what the homeowner is willing to accept.

When the buyer makes an offer, the homeowner cannot just accept the offer on his/her own. He has to take the offer to his bank and make an official request for a short sale status on the property. The bank then has the option to accept or reject the offer.

To get a short sale approved, the homeowner must file a number of documents including a hardship letter explaining why they are unable to repay the full amount of their mortgage. They will also have to give proof of their current financial status including pay stubs and tax returns. After the bank has reviewed the documentation, an appraiser has verified the full value of the property and the offer, they will make their decision.

When making a short sale offer, expect to have even closer scrutiny than normal. The bank will want to thoroughly vet you, calculate any risks they may be accepting and any potential opportunities.

Short sales are not the ideal solution for the homeowner, especially if they are suffering from financial difficulties, but it may be the best option. It also helps them to avoid foreclosure, which can be very damaging to their credit score. Thus, they can recover faster and will be in a better position to buy again in the future.

For the buyer, it can provide you with a property at a significant discount but at the same time, you will incur extra expenses that the homeowner usually has to pay. Expect to pay all the fees and charges that are connected to any home purchase. The cost includes agent commissions, which are normally paid by the bank, closing costs, inspections and so on.

How To Finance And Pay For A Rental Property

Deciding how much to invest, especially if it is for the first time, is a combination of mathematics, finances, and a budget. How much should be budgeted for an investment property? How much is charged for rent? How much does an investor want to have as a cash flow?

How Much to Invest

- Plan on putting at least 20% of the purchase price of the rental property and get prequalified for a loan. There's a lot of competition for investment properties being ready for submitting an offer

- Calculate between 5-10% of the annual rent in the event of a vacancy

- Property and liability insurance

- Taxes on the property

- The cost of repairs over the course of ownership

- Attorney fees, accountant, property management company

- Permits, code compliance with the area municipality

Once you have an idea of the strategy that you would like to work with, it is time to talk about financing. If you are able to save up the amount of money that you need, this is the best option. You won't have to worry about paying the bank at all and there is no need to worry about interest adding up.

You can start making more income right from the beginning, minus the unexpected expenses and some taxes and insurance. Of course, most people who are ready to start investing in real estate don't have this much money saved up (it is pretty expensive to purchase a house or an apartment building for example) so they will need to find some form of financing to help them to make the purchase.

As you get into this journey, it is a good idea to look at various funding sources to find out which one will offer you the best terms and the best rates to help save you money. Also, make sure that your credit score is in good order, that you feel out the applications thoroughly, and even have a marketing plan in place to show potential investors that you are serious about your new business.

Some of the best sources of financing that you can use to help fund your rental properties include:

Banks and credit unions

One of the first places that you will stop in order to finance your rental property is a bank or credit union. These have a long application process, but they have the best terms when it comes to interest rates, security, and length of the loan so that you can save some money. You will most likely need to go in and fill out a lengthy application, provide proof of income, have a good credit score, and even show your marketing plan to prove that you are serious about this investment.

Banks can be tough to get funding from because so many people come to them for help and they want to make sure that they are going to get their money back. If you want to increase your chances of getting the funding that is needed, make sure that you fill out the application completely and that you provide all the information that is asked for. Picking out a bank or credit union that you use is also a good idea because they are familiar with you and will be more willing to work with you.

Independent investors in your area

In some cases, there are independent investors who are looking to grow their portfolio, but they are not able to do some of the work of real estate on their own. They may be willing to provide you with some of the funding that you need in order to earn a good return on their investment while letting you take care of all the hard work. They basically take the risk while you are doing the work.

These investors can be a great resource for you, and it is very important to act professionally when talking to them. Have a presentation set up that shows what your goals are and the terms that you would like to use when paying back the amount that they loan. Be ready for some negotiations so that both parties are able to reach an agreement that is satisfactory.

Family and friends

If you have some friends and family who are willing to help you out or who would like to start investing themselves without having to do the work, this can be a good place to get some funding for your ventures. Often these are going to offer some good terms because these are people you know.

When working with people you know about funding for your rental properties, make sure that you set up some terms and conditions, such as how much interest you will pay them and when the full amount is due back, right from the beginning. Even though they are people you know, it is important to put these figures in writing so everyone is on the same page in terms of expectations and there aren't any hard feelings between the two groups.

Finding funding for the rental property, especially if you haven't built up any equity yet, can be an important step to taking care of your investment. There are many options to try and picking one that gives you the best terms is perfect for getting you on the right foot to success in this business and can even determine how much income you will get out of the whole process.

The Property Search

Once you have the financing in order and you know how much you will be able to get from the bank and how much you are able to afford, it is time to look for a property. There are several methods that you can use in order to find the right property that will be a good price, in a nice neighborhood, and will attract the tenants that you would like. Many beginners' like to work with a real estate agent because they know the area and can often find some of the best information about deals in the area and can help you determine if a property is right for your needs.

Places to look for homes

There are a variety of places you can search in order to find a property for your rental income. You do need to be careful with the homes you pick, though; just because they are nice doesn't mean they are priced competitively enough that you can make an income from the rent. But with some good researching skills and some patience, you will be able to find the perfect property. Some of the resources that you can use to find a good property include:

- Your realtor: many times those who are looking for a new property, whether to purchase for themselves or for an investment, will go with a realtor. The realtor knows a lot of information about your area and can find some of the properties that you may have missed.

- The MLS: one of the first places you should go to find a home. All homes that are listed with any of the agents in your area will be listed on this database. This can also be helpful if you are looking in a different town for the homes because you can just see which ones are listed nationally. Your realtor will often pick this option as well to help you find some of the properties that you want.

- Online home listing sites: in addition to the MLS, there are a few other places you can look to find homes that are available. Look on sites like auction.com, Zillow.com, and more to see if there are some good deals on the homes you would like to purchase.

- Driving around town: some of the best deals in purchasing real estate is to look for homes that are sold by the owner rather than by the realtor. Usually, the sellers have to pay their realtor a percentage of the sale, so this increases how much they will try to ask for the home. But for sale by owner homes have fewer expenses so that savings can be given to you.

• Networking: sometimes it is the people you know who can help you to find the right property. If you know a lot of people in the real estate industry and around town, you may hear some of the rumors about a home that may be coming for sale and at a good price.

You may be able to talk to them about purchasing the home before it even gets to the market. Some of the best sales in real estate never even get listed online or with an agent and if you are good at networking, you will be able to find them.

• Craigslist: Sometimes this can be a great place to start with finding the right rental property for you. Some for sale by owners are listed there because it is free to do the listing and can reach a large audience.

Be careful when using this option, though. Never send money to someone through craigslist and always go and take a look at the property ahead of time.

Finding the right property can take some time. You want to find a home that someone else would be willing to rent from you and you need to make sure that it is at a good price so you can still make an income. But if you look around at all these different options and keep your eyes open, you will find something that you really like.

Meeting your criteria

Before you get into a home, you should create a list of criteria that you would like the home to meet. How much will you be willing to pay for the property, how many bedrooms and bathrooms do you want, do you want it to have a basement, is there a backyard? You need to write all of this down before you even step foot into the first home on your search.

It is common to get into a home and fall in love with it, but it may be too expensive for your price range and you won't be able to rent it out and still make a profit. Or there may be so much work to it, it may be missing some things, or there are other issues that don't meet up with your criteria and could cost you a lot of wasted time and money.

Some of the requirements that you may want to stick with if you would like to purchase a home for a single family include a home that has three bedrooms, is near a school, and has both a yard and a garage. If you want to just have a smaller family or single people in the home, the criteria would change a little bit. Know what kind of customer you would like to work with because this will often determine what kind of property you decide to go with.

There are some times when you can vary off your requirements a bit, such as being slightly out of the neighborhood that you want to save some money, but for the most time, you should bring this list of criteria to all the house searches that you do. This helps you to keep on track and will help you to avoid getting a property that won't work for your rental needs.

Picking out the property that you will purchase can be an exciting time, but there are many things that you have to consider to make sure that you get the property that is nice, that will attract the right tenants, and will still be at a good cost so that you can pick a competitive rent and still make an income.

You need to take your time, run the numbers on each property, and make some important decisions to help protect your investment and get the right rental income to work for you.

Once you have been able to pick out a new property to use as your rental investment, it is time to make sure that the property is ready to rent out. You want to make sure that the property looks nice to a potential renter so that you can get them into the building, keep them comfortable so they stay in the property for longer, and ensure that you make some income off the work.

A good place to get started is to look at the property and pretend that you would be moving in here. What are some basic things that you can do to the property that would help to make it more comfortable?

What are some of the things that you see that may turn people off of the property? You can make some of these changes in order to get the property to look nice and pleasing to a potential renter.

To make the potential renter more comfortable in the property, make sure to take care of the following things:

- Fix anything that is broken

In most cases, if the property was a good deal, it is because there are at least a few things that you must fix and clean up around the home. You may need to spend some time painting some of the rooms, fixing some of the spots that are inside the wall or changing out the appliances that don't work. These are things that you should have added into your consideration when choosing whether to get this property or not because it is going to cost you a little more and this should be determined by the price.

If there are a lot of things inside of the property that are worn down and broken, it is going to be hard to get others to want to live inside of it. Make sure that it all looks nice and neat and fix anything that is broken and doesn't work as nicely as it should.

Make sure the home meets all codes

Every home needs to meet certain codes before you are able to rent that property to others. If you don't fix some of the code violations, or you don't get the new violations fixed as quickly as you can, it is possible for the tenant to sue you and that could be the end of your investment.

You should be able to avoid most of these problems by doing an inspection before you made the purchase so that will save you a little bit of a headache. With that being said, if you own the property for some time, some new violations that come up later on and you need to get them fixed as quickly as possible.

Even once you get a tenant into the property, it is a good idea to schedule in some regular checks on the different features of the home. this could include some things like the heater, the water, and the electricity. This helps you to check out each of these items to make sure they are up to the proper codes.

Make sure that you tell the tenant when you plan to do this, you can't just walk into the property because the tenant does have some rights. But if you give them a written notice ahead of time or add it into the lease, then the tenant will know when you are coming and you can make sure the home is safe.

Change the locks

Any and all locks that are in the home and the garage need to be changed. This includes the ones for all the doors in the property, the mailboxes, the sheds, the gates, and even the garage if there are keys to this. This should be done after you make the purchase and after each tenant leaves. This helps you to know that only the tenant and you have the right keys to this property so that no one else is able to get into the property.

Clean the carpets

It is very much worth your time to call in a professional to help you to take care of those carpets. There is so much that can get into the carpets over time from bad smells, stains, and more that a professional carpet cleaner who does a full steam, as well as a shampoo of the carpets, will be able to massively enhance the overall look of the house.

In some cases, you may choose to do some of this carpet cleaning on your own, but it is really going to make a difference if you hire a professional to help you get this done.

You may want to consider doing this each time that a tenant moves out of your property. This will make sure that all of the messes that they do to the property are taken care of and that the home looks really nice again when a new potential tenant comes in to look at it.

It doesn't take too much time to get the carpets done, but it can make a huge difference in how you find a new tenant.

Do some of the yard work

While the inside of the property is very important, don't underestimate the importance of taking care of the outside of the home as well. Your potential tenants want to feel comfortable on the property and if you leave it looking run down and a big mess on the outside, it is not going to matter how nice the inside looks. Luckily, making some changes to the landscaping and doing some yard work doesn't have to cost you a lot of money.

First, start with mowing the lawn, trimming any bushes and trees that may be a bit overgrown, pull out the weeds, and fix anything that you see is broken, if you notice there are a lot of plants that look dead or dying, pull them out.

You can even add in some other greenery and some flowers to make the home look more inviting. Don't forget to spray of the sidewalks to get the dirt to leave, keep leaves out of the yard, and just do some little fixes to make the home look nicer.

Change out the filters

If the home has been empty for some time, it is a good idea to change out the filters. You would be surprised at how dirty these things can get in no time and they really do affect how the ventilation system will work in your home. Before a new tenant moves in and on regular intervals afterward, make sure to clean out the vents and the area around them to keep the system working well.

Disposable filters are the best because you won't have to clean these out and most landlords find these are the easy ones to maintain.

Clean the interior

A good cleaning in the home can make a big difference on how nice it looks. It is best to go with a professional service to do this so that they can get the grime and the dirt that is hidden in the home, but the potential tenant may be able to notice. The walls should be wiped down well, the windows cleaned, and some care should be given to cleaning the appliances. Mop the floors or carpet clean your carpets. This does take a lot of time, but your tenant is definitely going to notice.

Add some more lights

Some tenants are not too thrilled with a home that doesn't have a lot of lights in it because it does make it hard to see inside the property and can make your property look smaller. If you notice that some of the light bulbs have gone out in the home, make sure to get them replaced.

Add some extra lamps in some rooms that may not have as many lights or windows and keep the curtains opened up so that the natural light can come through. In some cases, you can find brighter bulbs that will help to make the room look better and if you need to paint a few of the rooms, go with lighter colors to help with this.

Don't forget those ceiling fans

Never forget to spend some time cleaning the tops of the ceiling fans. These are often dusty and bad in no time and if a potential tenant sees this, it can look bad. First, get a wipe and learn how you should clean the tops and the sides of the fans. Then double check to make sure they are working or if it is time to replace some of the blades for your tenants.

Check the screens

Now it is time to check on your doors and windows. If these don't have some screens in place already, it is worth your time to invest in a few. You just need to measure out the space that you have available and then go to a local store to find the best screen replacements for your needs. Many homeowners want to be able to open up these windows without dust and bugs getting inside.

If the home already has some doors and windows inside, you need to inspect all of these. If there are holes, tears, and rips that you are not able to repair pretty quickly, it is a good idea to get them replaced. Also, you should check around the edges to see that all of these screens fit into their respective places properly. Wipe down all of the edges so that they look clean and nice.

Spray for the pests

Depending on how old the home is, how long it was sitting empty before you made a purchase, and even the area you live in, it is important to spray for pests. Sometimes there are pests inside and they try to make this their new home.

Even if someone is already living in the home or lived in it when you made the purchase, it is a good precaution to go through and spray for these pests to keep the home safe.

These are mostly little fixes that you will be able to do to make the home look nicer and to ensure that you are able to rent it out at a good price. They may be little things, but they are going to make a big difference to a potential tenant who wants the home to look nice and neat.

Chapter 4:

How To Repair And Maintain Rental Properties?

The management, repairs, and maintenance of a rental property can be daunting, inconvenient, time-consuming, frustrating, and a headache. That being said, let's review all that it takes to manage and maintain a rental property.

When an investor buys a property, they become a landlord. All the responsibility falls on their shoulders. It is an investment and the purpose is to have it create a positive cash flow, along with all the other benefits in real estate rental ownership. It is also supposed to offer a tenant a good place to live.

From the moment the rental becomes available to the public, the rental process begins, listed below.

- Make sure the property has all needed repairs done and is code compliant to be a rental property.

- List the rental on the market either with a real estate agent or on various social media websites and/or the local newspaper.

- Make appointments to meet prospective renters at the property.

- Meet prospective renters and show the rental. Answer questions and concerns.

- Hand out applications.

- Review applications submitted. The investor may have to go through a few applications before being satisfied with one that they feel will pass. If the application appears promising, such as employment and salary, the next step is

- Screening the tenant/Background check – if the background check passes, the rental is offered to renters.

- Sign the contract.

- Collect the security deposit(s) and first month's rent.

- Hand over the keys to the new tenant.

- Collect the rent each month.

- Attend to any maintenance issues over the course of the tenancy (and they usually always happen on the weekend).

- Follow up on any complaints made by neighbors, HOA, or authorities about a tenants' disruptive behavior.

- Dealing with non-payment of rent or continued partial payments of rent.

- Destruction to the property by tenants and/or pets.

- Evicting the tenant – having a 3-day pay or quit notice served and legally evicting the tenants if no payment is made after three days.

- File court documents for eviction.

- Have documents served on tenants.

- Eviction process usually can take anywhere from 30-45 days. If court calendars are full and any holidays occur during this time, it could take up to 60 days to evict. This tie up the property. It cannot be re-rented until vacant. This negatively impacts cash flow and finances.

- Inspect the property after it is vacant. Repair any damages to the property. If tenants, their pets, or anyone associated with the tenants (friends and family) caused damage to the property, deductions can be made from the security deposit to pay for it.

- Itemize any deductions made to the security deposit and send a letter, certified mail, to former tenants along with a check for the remainder of the deposit. If the damage and cleanup are extensive, it may necessitate that the entire deposit is used to remedy the condition and bring the property to the level of becoming rentable again. The security deposit may not cover all of the damage, and repairs may have to be paid out-of-pocket by the investor.

- Repeat the process all over again.

Some investors are handy with repairs and can make them without calling a handyman to do the fixing. However, not all are painters, electricians, plumbers, or roofers. They will probably have a network of licensed professionals who specialize in those types of repairs.

Hire a Property Manager/Management Company

If an investor wants to keep an arms distance from the entire landlord process, then they usually hire a property management person or company to manage their properties.

The responsibility does not lessen for the investor. They still have to make the ultimate decisions about the property. However, the time-consuming process is handled by another party whose sole responsibility is to execute all the aspects of managing and maintaining the investor's property.

A property manager or management firm usually charges 10 percent of the monthly rent for a single family home, and 4-7 percent for properties with 10 units or more.

The property manager or a management company set the rents on the properties to attract renters, collect the monthly rent, and adjust the rent for the next lease period according to the laws of the state or municipal laws.

Knowledge of all state and municipal landlord/tenant laws is the responsibility of a property manager.

In speaking with an experienced property manager who resides in South Florida, she gave a few insights into what it takes to successfully manage and maintain properties. Over her 21 years of experience, she has managed single family homes, fourplexes, and townhouses.

As a property manager, whether a small business, one person shop, or as a full staff management company, it is the responsibility of a property manager to keep the investor's investment managed, maintained, and in good working condition.

This is not always easy, because when asked what the hardest issues are in managing and maintaining a property, she stated there were a few that jumped out immediately.

The Tenants – some tenants will call for every little thing that happens at the property. A light bulb blew out in the refrigerator or in the bathroom. Or the tenant never changes the air conditioning filter, yet complains that the property is hot, and the air conditioning is not functioning properly.

The property manager must either send someone to remedy the problem or go out to the property themselves, purchasing a few light bulbs and air conditioning filters along the way, for the tenant's use.

Hiring a Handyman – having a few telephone numbers for a handyman is a must. They are usually called for the small repairs that are needed. A garbage disposal or toilet is stopped up, window blind needs to be replaced, or a door or doorknob keeps sticking. These are a few of the types of repairs they handle.

The problem with some handymen is that they say they will come and do the job, and some of them don't show up. Not only do they not show up, but they also don't even call to say they will be late or cannot make it that day.

Most times, when a repair has been requested, the tenant is at work and gives the property manager permission to enter the property with the handyman to fix the problem. When a handyman does not show up, it is very frustrating for the property manager who is waiting for them to arrive to let them in. The result is the problem is not fixed, the property manager's time is wasted, and the tenant comes home and finds that the repair had not been done.

The recommendation from the property manager is she will let it go the first time. If it happens again, she deletes their number from her phone.

Who Decides Repairs and Costs

As stated before, an investor usually has a network of people who help in managing and maintaining their investment. For the most part, the decisions on how the property is managed, and who does any rehabilitation or repairs falls on the investor.

However, the property manager can be called upon to recommend one of their contacts to do repairs or rehab, such as remodeling and upgrading kitchens and bathrooms, roofing, electrical, or plumbing repairs.

An experienced property manager usually knows the best people at reasonable rates and will hire them with the investor's consent. The investor is their client and the property manager wants to keep the investor happy and retain them as a client.

How Contractors Get Paid

A contractor, especially those who are in business for themselves, like to be paid on time. Many contractors ask for a deposit for their service before they begin the work. They don't like to run after the investor for payment. If such a case happens, the contractor, or the management company who hired and paid the contractor, can put a lien on the property until they are paid. This is called a mechanics lien.

In order to be able to pay contractors on time, it is suggested that a company checkbook be available to the property manager, to write checks for the services rendered by the various contractors and vendors that do work on the property. (If paid on time, a contractor will remember the investor's property and the investor as someone who pays on time. A fast pay gets good service).

Profit & Loss Reporting

The property budgets are managed by the property manager.

The property management company is responsible to submit a Profit & Loss (P&L) statement to the investor. This can be done quarterly, bi-annually, or annually at the preference of the investor.

The P&L will outline all the financial activities of the property. For example, a quarterly P&L will show how much rent was paid over the three months, deductions for any repairs done at the property, supplies purchased for the property (remember the light bulbs and air conditioning filters), any payment to contractors or handyman for repairs, etc. This information will help the investor when tax time rolls around. The property manager can file the taxes for the property if the investor so wishes.

It is up to the manager to make detailed notes of all repairs and have invoices to back up all expenditures. An investor wants to know where the money is spent. They want to maintain their cash flow. All repairs and costs have to be approved by the investor. Only extreme emergencies can a manager decide to have a repair done without the consent of the investor. If the tenants are in danger, or the physical structure of the property is a concern, the repair can be made, saving the property and removing the potential danger to the tenants. The repair is not considered unauthorized and the investor will approve.

Evictions

They are not pleasant for property managers either. However, property management companies handle evictions all too frequently and follow the legal procedure to evict a tenant for non-payment of rent, or other issues that breach the rental contract. The investor is always consulted prior to beginning any legal proceedings, but the execution is left to the management company.

Some management companies handle all the filings and have someone representing the management company appears in court for the eviction proceedings.

Others, especially smaller companies or one person who manages the property, will hire an eviction lawyer to handle all the proceedings. This, of course, is for a fee, but a smaller management company can't afford to sit in court when they have a number of other issues they have to attend to during the day. The fee is part of doing business and is added to the investor's P&L.

Whether an investor is a hands-on person who is handy in doing repairs and has time to perform all the functions required as a landlord, or is a busy investor who doesn't know how to wield a hammer or use a screwdriver, nor wants to, there are options in managing and maintaining their investment rental property.

A real estate rental investment takes time and money to maintain and upkeep. With the focus on preserving the property, being proactive with repairs, and keeping the rental as a safe and healthy environment for their tenants, will allow an investor to reap the profitable rewards for their efforts.

Managing the Property

If you are planning to flip the house and sell it after the rehab, the next step will be to find a realtor and get the newly refurbished home out on the market. The sooner you do this, the faster you'll be able to get a return on your investment. However, if the market takes a slump and you can't find a buyer within a reasonable amount of time or you choose not to sell as you set up your own personal real estate empire. If either of these is the case, your next step is to turn your property into a rental.

Investing in rentals is a great way to build up a steady flow of cash that will cover all the expenses you still have hanging over your head after the project has completed. Many people refer to rentals as truly passive income, but that is not always the case. If your decision is to manage the property yourself, then you will be working quite a bit in order to maintain the property, deal with maintenance issues, and collecting rents.

If you are new to the rehab game, you'll start out managing the task yourself. But if you plan on buying more properties you'll have a decision to make. Should you hire a property manager or should you continue to do the work yourself? The decision is a personal one, but it starts with taking a look at yourself in the mirror.

Should You Hire a Manager?

There is a lot of work involved in managing rentals. It is not just about collecting rents and cleaning up after a tenant moves out. In addition to maintaining the property, there is a lot of paperwork involved. You'll have to file tax reports, hire workers, manage collections, interact with the tenants, deal with complaints, and several other things here and there.

You need to be sure that you are the kind of person that can actually do this kind of work. If you are going to do the work yourself, it will be a real job that you will have to report to on a regular basis, especially if you plan on having more than one property. You will have to be quick on managing problems, tough enough not to buy into tenant's sad stories, and fearless enough not to back down when problems arise.

This may be easy to do for the first few properties but after a while, it will consume all of your time and energy. Management companies are skilled at this kind of impersonal work. They are much better at screening tenants, getting them to pay on time, and already have a team of workers who will be ready to address any maintenance issues quickly.

You cannot underestimate the value of a management company for your business. They know how to screen tenants, you'll have more reliable tenants living on your property who will be paying their rent on time. They are better able to handle maintenance issues in a timely manner. You won't have to worry about your property getting run down and losing its value. Since they know how to handle complaints efficiently, you are more likely to have tenants who are happy and won't be looking to move to another location.

You also have to consider the type of properties you are invested in. If your properties all consist of single-family homes then your management skills may be sufficient. However, if you've invested in commercial properties or multi-family dwellings then being a hands-on manager may turn out to be too time-consuming for you. Let's look at all the aspects of management that you will have to deal with.

Property Evaluation

Managers can evaluate the property after a tenant vacates. You will need to walk through the property to assess what is still in working order, what may need repair, or what work needs to be done before the next tenant moves in. A property management company will have their own workers to do this for you and will usually give you a pretty reliable estimate on costs.

Rent Figures

Managers can help decide on how much rent to charge. You may believe that your rents are reasonable, but a property manager is more in tune with what the market will bear. However, you can still maintain control over this area as a property manager's goal is to rent the units fast and may not be willing to wait for a reasonable price. (They don't get paid for vacancies.)

Screening Tenants

A manager must screen the tenants and select the best one. Screening can present quite a few headaches. This involves placing ads for the property, showing it, checking references, preparing leases, doing credit checks, and collecting money. They are less emotional about the task and will not accept a tenant purely on the money they have in hand. They will select the best tenants of all the applicants because they want to make sure that the tenant will stay and pay.

Collecting Rent

Property manages will make sure that the rents are collected on time. They will not hesitate to charge late fees or let the rent slide. This sets a bad precedent and the tenants will eventually not make paying their rent a priority and may even stop paying completely. If they fall too far behind, managers will start the eviction process.

Check on the Property's Condition

Managers will perform periodic checks on the property to ensure that it is being taken care of properly. In many leases, there is a clause that has been included allowing for an annual or bi-annual check to ensure that the property is being maintained properly. Property managers will notify tenants and do the inspection to make sure the house is not being damaged in any way.

Handling Evictions

No one likes the idea of an eviction. It is never pleasant but at times it is necessary. The manager will work to get the tenant out on good terms as much as possible. If they cannot, they will take on this unpleasant task without hesitation. This will likely cost you more money but not nearly as much as having a deadbeat tenant on your hands.

Thorough Inspection

Managers can have properties thoroughly inspected before they are rented. Even after rental, expect that things will break and must be fixed. Regular maintenance before, during, and after a tenant moves in is their responsibility. They are available 24/7 to make sure that these problems are addressed for the benefit of both you and the tenant.

Paperwork

Managers also handle all of the necessary paperwork associated with the property. These include accounting and taxes. They will keep track of how much rent you've collected, how much maintenance costs you, manage your profit/losses and supply you with a year-end report.

You may choose to start out managing the property yourself, but as your business grows, you are likely going to be much more interested in hiring a property manager to handle much of the grunt work for you.

Paying Your Property Manager

Managing properties is not an easy job. There are a lot of small details that need to be taken care of. This doesn't mean that all properties will be equally hard to manage. Not all the tenants will pay their rent late, the same way, not every unit will require a steady flow of repairs, and issues are not going to come up in every case. In fact, there are properties that will be successfully rented out for years without ever having a problem.

So, how much should you expect to pay your property manager? In short, every case is going to be different. Many people feel that hiring a manager may not be worth it, or they've had bad experiences with ineffective managers in the past. As the owner of the property, the tenant should recognize that you make all the decisions, which can make it hard for you if a problem comes up. Most people want managers to handle complicated situations like evictions, screening, and handling complaints. If you don't mind dealing with these possible problems, you may not have to worry about hiring a manager.

However, you don't want to wait until you have a problem to hire a manager. If you do decide to hire one, it means you can expect to pay a percentage of your rents collected every month to cover their fees, which usually range from 8 to 12% every month. From that, some management companies may have additional fees. It is worth negotiating exactly what you want them to do and how much you are willing to pay for it.

Investment of Time

Your decision to hire a manager will depend a great deal on how much work is involved. Managing a lot of properties will naturally take a lot of time. However, if you only have one property, it may not be worth it for you to hire someone. It may only take an investment of a few hours every month to go over, cut the grass, or take care of the regular maintenance duties, collect the rents, and make bank deposits.

The need comes up when you have multiple rental properties to manage. A few hours per month now increases to a few hours per week or more. Managing multiple problems might result in things getting out of hand very quickly. If you do not have the time to deal with them, then it's quite clear that best thing for you to do is hire a manager.

If you think you can handle the extra workload, there are several strategies that can help you to keep on top of things. You need to be organized, with a system that schedules when you need to collect your rent and keep a record of who paid. When you are dealing with multiple properties, this can seem like a breeze at first, but in time, other priorities might be put first. When that happens, if you want to keep your business solvent, seriously consider hiring a manager.

Renting Out Your Property

For onlookers, renting out a property seems pretty easy. Set a price, place an ad, and get a tenant, collect the rent and you're done. Well, that's the basics but there is a lot more involved than that. Let's go through the steps on how to rent out your property in the most efficient manner

First, determine how much rent you can reasonably expect for your property. This can be a tricky process because the amount of rent is not determined just by the value of the house but also by what the market can stand. In most areas in the country, how much you got for selling your property as a matter of public record, but how much you got in rent is not. The only way you can get a ballpark figure of what everyone else is paying is to study the active rental ads for vacancies in your area, or you can talk to a rental agency.

Deciding this figure should be determined even before you decide to purchase the property. It should have a bearing on how much you're willing to pay to buy and renovate if you don't reasonably expect to get that money back and some in rent, it is really not worth making the investment in the first place.

As you go through the rental listings in your area, take note of all the properties that are similar to yours and then check back periodically to see how long they took to rent out. You can usually tell when a property is rented because the ad will be removed. You can call to double check just to make sure.

A property manager knows what is a reasonable rent to ask, especially if they are responsible for managing a lot of properties. Make sure you screen your managers carefully though, some will take a shortcut and undercut your rent just so they can get money faster.

If you're still not sure how to price your rental you can get a rent report from rentrange.com, which will do the comparison work for you. Registering with them will give you a good picture of how much the rents are going for in your area and what reminders you should be aware of specifically in your area.

Pricing Your Property

Once you have the range of rentals in your area, you have to come down to a specific figure. There are several different methods investors do.

1. Some price the rents at the top range of what the market will accept, hoping to find a renter who is willing to pay for quality.

2. Others price just below the market, so they get a lot of applicants and can choose the best one.

Which strategy you choose depends on your preference. With option one, you get a renter who doesn't mind paying a little extra for a nicer home, but with option two, you know who gets your place. There are pros and cons to both methods.

Once you've determined the rent for the property, you need to place an ad. This can be anything from sticking a for rent sign in the window or posting on an online classified ad space. Before you do this, you need to learn how potential renters seek out properties in your area. Some will go to online sites like Zillow first while others will turn to ads on Craigslist, a local flyer, or through other channels. You need to be where the renters are looking otherwise, it could take months for the right tenant to find your property.

Showing the Property

Once potential renters see your ad, you now have to show the property to them. You can either have an open house where they can walk in freely or have them schedule an appointment for a walk through. The open house frees up a lot of your time and can possibly attract more potential renters who never saw your ad. The scheduled walk through gives you more one on one time with the individuals to find out what kind of tenants they may be.

When interest is shown, you can start the application process. You can find many standard rental applications online that you can adjust to your needs. You can also have your lawyer draw up one specifically designed for your unique qualifications. Most landlords charge a rental fee that will cover this expense and a credit check. A good potential tenant won't have any problem with paying the fees and it is a way to make sure that the applicant is serious about renting your property.

It is important that you observe the person as he goes through the property. Study the application carefully. The goal is to learn as much as possible about them. The more they talk, the better the picture you'll get about how they will live in your place. Their application needs to be filled out thoroughly with no blank spaces, several verifiable references, and necessary information to check their credit. Always check references, especially for their last place of residence. Find out not just if they paid their rent on time but if they were a nuisance tenant or not. Did they destroy the place or were they responsible.

Employment verification is key. If they have only been working for a short period of time, which may be a cause for concern. However, if they have been on the job a long time it is evidence of a stable income.

Chapter 5:

How Do I Get To Dynasty Status?

The rental real estate market comprises of different types of property rentals from single family homes to apartment rentals. Depending on the type you own you will be targeting a specific corner of the housing market. Think about where your tenant pool will most likely look for rental vacancies and advertise your property rental there.

The 10 most commonly used marketing methods used to advertise rental vacancies

1. The "for rent" yard sign
2. Community newspapers
3. Online property rental ads

4. University campuses
5. Community news boards in local supermarkets
6. Newspaper classifieds
7. Let your social network of family, friends, colleagues know you have a property rental available
8. Existing tenants
9. Social media
10. Rental real estate agencies

You can take care of marketing your property rental on your own or engage the services of a real estate agency. Consider the advantages below of each before deciding which option works best for your needs.

Benefits of marketing your own property rental

- You save on management company fees.
- You free up time to devote to other property investment activities.
- There are many different methods to advertise your property.

Advantages of using a real estate agency to find tenants

- You utilize the experience and knowledge of industry professionals.
- Realtors have a readily accessible database of applicants looking for rental property.
- Realtors can show potential tenants the available property as well as screen applicants for you.

What your marketing copy should entail

It is the words you use that provide vital information to a prospective tenant. Photographs will attract interest but a carefully-worded advert or listing will tell a tenant what he or she wants to know.

When creating marketing copy be specific about the number of rooms, parking spots etc. Include adjectives that are appealing such as 'sunny' 'spacious or well-sized' 'luxurious' 'stainless' 'landscaped' 'granite' 'updated'

Your advertising copy needs to entice prospective tenants which mean you need to compile a list of desirable features a would-be tenant will look for. To make sure you leave nothing out consider a walk-through the property as you make your list. This way you will leave nothing out.

Highlight the positive points of your rental like a balcony or landscaped garden while also mentioning the negatives like no garage for parking. This way you will only attract potential tenants who are interested in what you are offering.

You have heard the well-used refrain 'a picture tells a thousand words' before. Photos are a huge selling point for prospective tenants. A property vacancy ad (in print ads or online) with an image is more effective in generating interest. It is, therefore, a good idea to use a professional photographer (especially one that is experienced in photographing real estate) or good quality camera to take photos of your property to post online or accompany advertising listings or even to share on social media. Your camera phone is not good enough. You want the high resolution capabilities of a top quality digital camera to work for you. Make use of editing software to enhance images but take care not to misrepresent what your rental looks like.

You can also create a virtual video tour of your property rental that can be viewed and shared on social media.

Most tenants will want to know the following details:

- Location
- Size of rental
- Rent and security deposit required

- Number of rooms
- Utilities
- Any policies applicable (no smoking or no pets)
- Your contact information

Think about the attractive features your rental has that a potential tenant may look for. Once again, knowing who your target market is will help. Rope in a friend or two to help. Different pairs of eyes may notice something you don't.

Does your property rental have any of the following attributes?

- Home office space
- Laundry room
- Fireplace
- Balcony
- Swimming pool
- Air conditioning

Students will want to know if the property is close to bus routes and other public transport facilities? Is it close to shopping and entertainment hubs? Families will care about nearby hospitals, clinics and schools. What major roads and routes are within easy proximity?

Screening Your Tenant Applicants

Your ability to screen your tenant applicants in order to choose the right one for your rental property will determine your overall experience as a landlord. Do it poorly, and you may end up with a tenant straight from the bowels of hell, and if you do it right, you can end up with an angel of a tenant and enjoy a relatively stress-free - and profitable if I may add - stint as a landlord. But this activity is also governed by Fair Housing Laws, so you must know how to do it in accordance with such laws.

As a landlord, you'll need to have a printed or written Tenant Selection Plan that details your criteria for approving tenant applications for your rental property. The selection plan must include guidelines for occupying your property, your policy for the availability of the property, and criterions you will use for accepting tenant applications (these include income, employment history, credit scores, etc.). Also, detailed explanations of each criterion, a general outline of the tenant application process, and a statement that says you adhere to all applicable Fair Housing Laws. And equally important, you must furnish your applicants a copy of your Tenant Selection Plan even before they fill up and sign your rental application forms.

Next, you must also prepare your rental application form. This document is essential because aside from information gathering, it also serves as your official authorization for running background and credit checks later on. Let's talk about information gathering first.

You must not ask your tenant applicants questions about disabilities whether mental or physical. And while you may ask questions concerning lawsuits and substance use (alcohol, drugs, etc.), such questions in the application form must be limited. Perfectly acceptable questions to ask in the application form include those that can help you gather information regarding the applicants' past money judgments, evictions, bankruptcies, and their reasons for leaving their current landlords.

Financial Background Checks

This is probably the most crucial part of screening your tenant applicants. Remember, being a landlord means you're a small business owner and as such, you're in it to make money and not lose it. If you screw up this part of tenant applicant evaluation process, your risk of ending up with a delinquent, non-paying tenant increases substantially. Worse, you might even end up with a money laundering or criminal tenant, which will not only be a financial problem but a huge legal one too. But you must do this right, i.e., in compliance with Fair Housing Laws.

Before even running any checks, you must remember to have them fill up and sign your rental application form first, which should include a clause that authorizes you to run background, financial, and credit checks on the applicants. If you conduct credit or background checks without any authorization, you can face serious legal problems. So do it right the first time by having them fill up and sign your rental application form first before running checks on them.

There are three critical steps to verifying your tenant applicants' income or financial capacity: Securing vital financial documents, verifying employment with the employer (if employed), and running a credit check.

Securing Financial Documents

The first process of evaluating your prospective tenants' financial capacity is to ask for copies of key financial documents from them, such as last three months' bank statements (if self-employed), their W2 forms, and last three months' payslips (if employed). You will also need to request a copy of the prospective tenants' Form 4506-T form IRS, which is practical but equally effective as Form 4506.

Employment Verification

If your prospective tenant is an employee, another step needs to be taken, which is to make sure that he or she's really working for the employer indicated on the application form. For this, you can go straight to their employer considering the signed application form includes authorization to conduct background checks, including employment. If for some reason the employer refuses to divulge information on the grounds that they don't know if you're authorized to do so, you can either ask the applicant to call them and vouch for you or show them a copy of the signed rental application form that includes your authorization.

Credit Checks

This final step will help give you an idea of your prospective tenants' true financial condition and capacity, which can go a long way towards helping your protect your rental property and successfully make money off it. Applicants with very good credit scores (excellent credit history, timely payment of bills) have much lower risks of not being able to pay rent than those with low scores.

A credit check will give you information that can help you get an excellent estimate if an applicant is able to pay the monthly rent on time or not successfully. Some of the information included in a credit check - which may vary according to the agency hired - include:

- Confirmed personal details such as full name, addresses (both current and past), birthday, employers (current and past), spouse's identity, and social security number

- Credit history including outstanding loans (including the type of loans, amount of loans, available credit limit, the age of loans, last two years' payment history, co-borrowers if any), credit card accounts, and bank accounts

- Public records such as financial judgments and tax liens vs. the applicants, bankruptcies filed, and reported evictions

- The names of people or institutions that have asked for a credit report on the applicants within the last 12 months

- For some reports, even the applicant's credit or FICO score may be included.

Information Needed For a Credit Check

To successfully conduct a credit check, you must know the applicant's full name, birthday, address in the last two years, social security number, current employer (if employed), and current or most recent landlord. And as mentioned earlier, you'll need to be authorized to run the check, which should already be included in the signed rental application form submitted to you.

Turning Down an Applicant, Legally

It's in your best interests to accept an applicant that meets your criteria, which should've been documented and given to your applicants before even filling up and signing an application form. But as the Highlander movie and television series always says, there can only be one approved tenant per property. This means you'll have to turn applicants down along the way. But the way you turn down applicants must also be compliant with Fair Housing laws. Otherwise, you're putting yourself at risk of being sued for "discrimination."

To avoid being sued for perceived discrimination, you shouldn't just tell your rental applicants that they didn't make the cut without giving them reasons why you're not renting the property out to them, even if you actually have legal reasons for doing so. Legal reasons that are not communicated won't cut it for you-you'll need to communicate it to them when you formally inform them of your decision to turn down their applications. And under the Fair Housing Act, you may not turn down rental applicants on the basis of nationality, skin color, disabilities, marital status, gender, religion or race.

You may turn down rental applicants for as long as you can prove that all applicants were evaluated equally and using the same criteria and process, and your basis for doing so should be a high probability that they won't be able to pay rent (based on financial records and credit checks) or if the rental applicants can pose serious security threats to the property and the neighborhood in which it's located. But even if you have the legal justification to turn applicants down, you must do it the "right" way too, especially if the basis for doing so are credit check results or other public records.

If your basis for turning down a rental applicant is because of unfavorable results of conducted credit checks, you must give the applicant an Adverse Action Notice, which is a federal requirement under Federal Fair Credit Reporting Act. This document tells the applicant that the application was turned down because of adverse findings or results of the credit check conducted on him or her. The contact details of the agency that ran the check must also be included in the notice to give the applicant the chance to access the report and if ever, contest it.

If the applicant responds to your notice saying that the credit check's information is not accurate, you can ask the person to contact the agency that prepared the report directly to contest the information. This is because you have no authority and basis for determining whether or not the information on the report is inaccurate, as well as to revise the report. It's your legal right to insist that in the absence of any revision, clarification or adjustment in the credit report prepared by the agency you hired, your decision stands.

If you turn down an applicant because of a dangerous criminal record, keep in mind that the records must show that the applicant has been convicted of dangerous crimes that can potentially put the property and the people living within the area at risk. Merely being arrested won't cut it when it comes to determining the qualifications of a rental applicant. Other restrictions per the United States Department of Housing And Urban Development:

- You can't use blanket statements or terms in your Tenant Selection Plan that says something like "applicants with criminal convictions will be turned down or rejected." because it's considered as a violation of the Fair Housing Act's provisions on discrimination.

- You must provide the applicant with a denial letter as well as instructions on how he or she can secure a copy of the report. Or record that you used as the basis for turning down the application if such information or record was the basis for your decision (the law doesn't require you to provide a copy of the report to the applicant).

To have a much easier time when it comes to rejecting rental applications correctly, the United States Land Protection Agency suggests that you make a standardized letter that you can give to rejected applicants, which contain a checklist of possible legal reasons for rejecting a rental applicant. As a landlord, you merely check the reason on the list for your decision to turn down an application. These reasons should include:

- Unacceptable rental offer price
- Inadequate income
- Inability to verify employment
- Poor credit history (if this is the reason, attach an adverse action letter)
- Pets
- Smoking
- The applicant provided false information on the application form
- Incomplete information on the application form
- Others

Having such a standardized letter already prepared can help you turn down rental applicants in a more time efficient manner because with a template on hand, you won't have to spend so much time crafting letters individually and responding to the complaints of rejected applicants. More importantly, such a letter provides the rejected applicants a proper and comprehensive explanation for the rejection.

Lastly, you have to remember that when it comes to approving rental applications for your property, you must do so on a first-come-first-served basis. And by this, the law doesn't mean the first applicant always wins. By first, the law means to say that the first qualified applicant. Even if an applicant was first in line, but it was proven that he or she's not qualified, his or her application can be rejected. Tell the rental applicant the real reason for them being denied, i.e., that even though they were approved or qualified to rent your property, someone else beat them to the draw by virtue of being first in line. If you have other rental properties, you can tell them to apply for those if they're interested.

Keep these in mind when you have to turn down your rental property's applicants. By keeping within these parameters and complying with legal requirements for doing so, you'll be able to protect yourself from the hassles of having to address discrimination claims against you.

Accepting Tenants

As mentioned earlier, the first QUALIFIED rental applicant or the first approved rental applicant is the one that should be accepted. And to avoid discrimination claims from disgruntled applicants, you should have a system for documenting receipt of an application and for objectively establishing who the first qualified rental applicant is.

An excellent way to do this is by through time stamping and providing the rental applicants with a time-stamped, photocopied version of their signed application forms. The time stamping establishes the date and time of the application form's submission while the duplicate copy, which must be time stamped as well and signed as received by you, gives them a hard copy or evidence that they filed their application at a specific date and time - a sign of goodwill if you may.

Another purpose for their copies of the application forms is leverage when a discrimination claim arises. When you give them the copy, you can ask them if the date and time of receipt stamped on their copies are accurate. So if they claim that they submitted it earlier, you can always refer to the fact that they confirmed the accuracy of the time stamp when they submitted the application form. It's an excellent way to protect yourself against rental applicants who have serious attitude problems.

Commercial Real Estate

Understanding the difference in commercial real estate and residential real estate investing is as simple as knowing the difference in a home that people live in and a business that people work in. When you are figuring out how to make money with commercial real estate, you need to find out what is going to be popular in your area. For example, if you live in a large city, it will be better to have office buildings as commercial real estate. If you reside in a small town or even in an area where there is a lot of factory work and production, you may be better purchasing and renting out things like where businesses are located. The commercial real estate that will be profitable will be dependent on the area that you are in – nearly every location is going to be different.

It is a good idea to learn about commercial real estate before you jump into it. You need to know what is selling, what is not renting out and what is going to work best for you. You should also know the specifics of commercial real estate in your area. Are there laws that govern what you can and can't rent out? Do you have to follow certain codes? Is there a limit to how many commercial buildings you own before you become a principal developer? All of these questions are ones that can't be answered by this book but will instead need to be figured out in a more local sense.

By reading this book, you will be able to figure out what type of property will be profitable for you, the amount that particular properties are worth and the best ways to finance the property. You can also learn the negotiation tactics that pros use so that you can try to make the most out of the process. It is a good idea always to figure out how you can benefit from the tax breaks and the deals that are sometimes found with commercial properties. Try your best, and you will be able to have the best experience possible with commercial real estate.

Having commercial real estate can be a hugely lucrative investment. Not only is it a career that you can benefit from in the now, but it is also something that will bring in residual income for years to come. When you find the right type of property and the right way to market it, there is very little work that you will have to do later on. It will give you the chance to continue to collect money for a period in the future – you'll be able to benefit from the work that you put into it.

Commercial real estate investment, while lucrative, can be a huge time and money investment. You will need to put a lot of work and capital into your commercial real estate so be sure that you are prepared for that. It is a good idea always to try and make sure that you are prepared as much as possible for the things that are going to come in the future. Always do your best and make sure that you are getting money built up and money that you can put aside to be able to contribute to your real estate investment.

Generating Leads on Commercial Properties

Knowing the right type of commercial property to invest in is only half of the process. Once you figure out what is going to work for you and what is going to make the most money, you need to work to make sure that you can find that property. To generate leads on properties that you can purchase and then turn around and rent out, you will need to take a few steps. These are important in that you can find the exact property that is perfect for you. They don't have to be followed in order; so try out different things until you find that perfect system that works for you.

A Lookout

You may consider hiring someone who can find the perfect commercial property for you. This is a bird dog or a lookout. They are trained to be able to find the best properties, and they will make the best decision possible for you. They can give you a list of properties and then you can make a choice from there on what you want to be able to purchase.

One thing that you should always do is hire a lookout who is a professional. With these professionals, you can give them a list of what you want in a property. They will then be able to look at the different things that you want and come back with a list of commercial real estates that is going to work for you.

This should be one of the last resorts for you. You will have to pay for this, and it will often be costly, so try to make sure that you can find something on your own first.

Land Developers

For many real estate investors, the end game is to become a land developer. This is where the real money is. While you are waiting at that point and just getting started, you can take advantage of these developers. It is a good idea to become friendly with developers. They are looking for people just like you – those who want to buy commercial properties. When you work with a developer, you will be sure that you are getting the best chance possible at the various options included in real estate investment for commercial properties.

The best thing about working with a developer is that they can often offer you deals that typical agents would not be able to offer you. Since they are the ones who developed the property, they will be in a better position to take money off of the bottom line so that you can get the best price possible.

Always make sure that, if you are working with a developer, it is someone who is reputable. You will be able to make more money and get a better deal if you work with someone who has a good reputation.

Simple Looking

Just driving around and looking at commercial properties for sale can be the best way to find a property. This is especially true in small towns and rural areas where there is not a lot of square mileage to drive around. You should make sure that you are looking at all of your options when you are looking around so that you can find out the different things that are included with the properties.

As you are looking around, be sure to figure out what the property entails – what is the cost of it, what do you think it is worth and where is it located? These questions will help you to make a decision later on; so, you may want to write down the answers for each of them according to the properties that you are looking at.

Take your time when you are looking. The first time that you are looking – just do that. Later on, you can contact real estate agents and try to find out more about the property. There are many steps to this process; so, be sure that you follow them.

Network with Others

There are many real estate networks available to investors even if you are in a small town with not a lot of major options. It is a good idea to always network with other people so that you can make the best choice possible. If you have a friend with a commercial property for sale, they will be more likely to sell to you than they would be to a random person; so, try to make business friends with everyone that you meet in the industry.

Networking is a great way to get a good start. Not only will it help you to figure out what type of property is going to work the best for you and also help to find that property, but it will also help you make contacts in other areas of real estate. From agents to inspectors and everything in between, a strong network is imperative to making a lot of money.

Try a Different Approach

Nearly all investors are doing the same things and trying the same tactics. If you want to be different, try something different. That could mean that you buy low-value properties and switch them up. It could also mean that you try to find properties that are in different areas. No matter what you are doing, you need to make sure that you are going to be able to figure out the right way to be able to get the best experience possible. It is also a wise decision to try and make sure that you are finding the best properties. There is a large profit margin that can come from finding the right property. When you are able to find that profit margin and are able to make it work for your investments, you will be able to get a much higher profit. It is something that real estate investors have been using for a long time and something that you can also benefit from in your investment business.

Determine the Value of a Property

To be able to make money from your commercial real estate investments, you will need to know the value of the property. The value takes everything into consideration – from the actual property worth to the amount that you can expect to bring in from the property over the years. There are many different things that you should take into consideration, and each of these will allow you to adjust the worth of the property. It is a good idea to know the value so that you can set the price to what you want to be able to do.

The Age of the Property

In some instances, newer properties will be worth more because of the options that they come with. In other instances, where buildings are better because they are vintage, older properties will be worth more. The age of the property will nearly always be taken into account when you look at the property; so, be sure that you are working to find out what is going to work for you.

Appraisal Value of It

You should always have the property professionally appraised. This is something that will show you what the true value of the property is. If you can do this before you buy the property, you will have a better chance of making more money off of it since you will know what the value of it is. If you do not do this before, it is important that you do it almost immediately after you have made the decision to purchase the property to rent out to others.

How Large It Is

The size of the space will determine how much money you should pay for it and how much money you will be able to get for it. Obviously, the larger the building is, the more expensive it will be for you to try and purchase. There are many instances when you might not need that space, though, so make sure that is something you are prepared for. You should always figure out how space is going to work for you and whether it will come in handy when you are renting the property out to other people for business use.

The Demand for Property like It

There will be a different amount of demand for different properties depending on the area that you are in. For example, some properties will cost much more in different areas because of the way that the properties are set up. It is a good idea to make sure that you are getting what you can out of the properties so that you know what the demand for each of the properties is in your area. It is a wise decision to be able to help people figure out what they are looking for and what they can do with various property options.

What It Can Be Used For

If you buy an office building, it will only be able to be used for offices. If you buy a warehouse, the same thing applies. You need to make sure that you are doing what you can to provide a building that is able to be used for different purposes. The more purposes a building has when it comes to your various options, the better chance you will have at making sure that the value is as high as possible. It is a good decision to choose a multipurpose building over one that only has a singular purpose.

The Zoning on It

Depending on where you live, there will be requirements on the zoning of your property. A property that is zoned in one way will not be able to be used for anything other than what it is zoned for. If you find a property that is not zoned for more than one thing, it may be a good idea to stay away from it. Zoning will depend on what the property can do, the area it is located and what you can put into it so that you can make sure that you are getting the best experience possible. Zone the property in a way that makes sense and the value will be changed.

Your Ability to Profit

The value of the property can change depending on how much you can profit from it as a rental. It is a good idea to try your best to figure out exactly what you are going to get from it on a monthly basis, a yearly basis and with a 5-year outlook on the property. You need to make sure that you are doing many different things with your property so be sure that you look at all of the aspects that will allow you to make the most amount of profit possible.

The Expected Life of the Property

There will come a time when you are no longer able to rent the property out. This is when the life of the property is over. It most commonly happens when the building gets old, when you are not able to make profits from it and when major things start happening to the property to decrease the value. Figure out when that point is and then calculate from when you are purchasing it until then. This is the expected life of the property, and it will make a difference with the way that you can rent it out. Be sure that you know this; and that will help to tell you the value.

Expected Value after Improvements

You should consider some of the improvements that you are going to make on the property. While you don't necessarily have to do a full flip on it or renovate it in the best way possible, you should consider the small improvements that you are going to make. From there, figure out what the value will be with the improvements that you are going to do to it. This will help you to understand the way that the property works.

Chapter 6:

What Properties Pack The Most Punch

Single Family Homes

Investing in single-family homes in many U.S. markets is a hot market to get into. Over the last three years, 30% of the single family homes purchased have been used as rental properties. (Sullivan, 2017). Investing in a single family home and turning it into a rental is the next type of property to invest in.

A Single Family Home is a detached, stand-alone house. The investor owns the home and the land it is on. Some single family homes are part of a Planned Unit Development (PUD). This is a community made up of single family homes or town homes. (Agranoff, 2012) There is an HOA and fees are paid monthly, quarterly, or annually. The fees cover the community roads or buildings that are part of the common area of the community. Some developments have play areas for kids and a community swimming pool.

Single-family homes are popular rentals and sought out by the public for a number of reasons. People will always need a place to call home, and will look for a property that fits their needs, and has a rent that is affordable. That being said, single-family homes are in high demand. Families with two to three children (and sometimes more) usually look for 3 bedrooms, 2 bathrooms home to rent. A family presents the possibility of their renting long-term while the children attend schools in the area and participate in community and school events.

Another attraction of single-family homes that attract renters is the ability for tenants to have pets. Town homes and condominiums allow pets, but many of them insist on a size cut-off for dogs. This means that a dog cannot weigh or be larger than the parameters set by the HOA. Some HOAs even restrict the number of pets a tenant can have, and certain breeds also fall under restrictions. A single-family home affords that a tenant can own a pet, and unless there is a size restriction stated in the lease, can own a dog without limitations.

Pets are covered by fees that are due at the beginning of a lease. If there is normal wear and tear to the property, and there is no damage caused by a pet, the fee can be made refundable at the end of the lease.

Properties that can be continuous rentals in college towns are another option for an investor to a profitable investment. College students who want to live off campus look for rental properties where a few people can split the rent. An off-campus residence is less cramped and confining than a dorm room to live in, making renting a house an attractive option.

Investors renting their property to any tenant should be very specific in the wording of the lease. In order to protect their investment, a lease usually should have stringent rules to abide by. Loud parties, noise, additional tenants who are not on the lease, causing disruption in the neighborhood, or damage to the property that is not normal wear and tear can be stipulated as a breach of the lease.

Townhouse and Condominiums

A townhouse and a condominium are the next types of real estate properties that an investor can invest in for rentals. There are differences between the two. Let's look at what they are.

Townhouse

A Townhouse is a style of construction. It is like a single family house, where the investor owns both the building and the land, but the difference between them is that a townhouse is not free standing and separate. There is ownership of the front and backyard, but it attached, sharing a common wall with to the next townhouse. Townhouses are usually built in a row and commonly are two stories, and don't have neighbors above or below the structure. A townhome can be a style of a condominium. (Agranoff, 2012) A townhouse can also be part of a PUD, with HOA dues used for upkeep of the community and community amenities.

Condominium

A Condominium (Condo) is where you and other members of the HOA jointly own the actual structure of the building, the common areas such as swimming pool, tennis courts, and any other amenities in the complex. The airspace and the interior of the structure are owned individually, but the building is not owned individually by any of the owners. (Agranoff, 2012)

There are a number of different structure styles that can be considered condominiums. A condo can be a ranch style attached units, 2 or 3 story units, or they can be an apartment style in a building. They can be one or two floors and can have a basement. Dependent on the configuration of the structure, there can be a neighbor above or below, or both.

When you own a condo, you do not own the land that the structure is on. A condo owner only owns the unit. It is taxed as an individual unit and sometimes a percentage of the common areas. Ownership of either a townhouse or a condominium refers to the type of ownership, not type of structure. (Agranoff, 2012)

Investing in a townhouse or condominium as a rental property comes with a number of rules and regulations. Covenants, Conditions, and Restrictions (CC&Rs) and HOA Bylaws.

The CC&Rs cover regulations on what can and cannot be done in a planned community. They are the rules of the neighborhood. Examples of what some of these are can be the following: (Loftsgordon)

- Garbage cans must be pulled off the street after trash pickup
- Cars must be parked at the curb
- Adults must accompany children to the swimming pool

HOA Bylaws are established by the Association to manage the Planned Unit Development (PUD). They are usually set up as a non-profit corporation. As a corporation, they have a Board of Directors with a President, Vice-President, Treasurer, and Secretary. It governs the business of the HOA. Some of the duties of the Board deal with HOA meetings and events. (Loftsgordon)

- How meetings are managed
- Duties of the officers of the Board
- Membership voting rights
- How many meetings the HOA will have over the year

Investing in a PUD or a condominium can present limitations for an investor. As stated before, there are limitations as to how many rental properties are allowed. Before investing, become familiar with the Association bylaws to check if the community has already reached the percentage level allowed for rentals.

Another aspect to consider is the HOA dues. Paying HOA dues are an owner's responsibility. Depending on the development, these dues can be high. The market value of rent that can be charged to a tenant may be diminished by the due's fees.

There are also special assessments to consider. A special assessment may be charged to the owners for a service that is not covered by the usual dues. Fees are shared proportionately based on the percentage of property owned. If an HOA has a healthy reserve account, it is possible that special assessments can be covered by the reserve. (Venzon)

Investigate what types of reserves are on hand. Speak to other owners to find out how the Association handles the reserve funds. Check the age and condition of the development. If it's an older development, there may be excessive repairs that need to be made and reserves may not cover them. Has the development met the quota of rental properties allowed? They may have and investing in a property that can't be rented is not how it will be profitable. (Venzon)

All of these points just covered will help an investor to decide whether or not investments in these types of real estate are worth it.

Investing in a below market value real estate property that can be rented relatively quickly after repairs and code inspections are passed, can be a sound and profitable investment. When the property is ready and goes on the market, the phone will start ringing with eager applicants. Proper screening of prospective tenants, a continuous cash flow, and all the other benefits attached to investing in rental properties, will make for profits an investor will want to repeat again and again.

Training Your Tenants to Pay on Time

There is no true way to "train" your tenants to pay their rent on time and to stay in the same location while they are renting with you, but there are some things that you can do that will make them more inclined to stay with you as a landlord. These things will allow you to work better as a landlord and will also give you the chance to make things better within your investment property that you are renting out. If you have tenants that are there for a long time, you can make more money from them instead of having to constantly cycle through other tenants who will not make it easy on you.

Be Courteous

You should always be courteous of your tenants. Do not make them think that you are their best friend but try to make it so that they are not completely intimidated by you. You should make sure that you are courteous to them and that you are always trying to make them as happy as possible with the things that you are doing. Remember that they are the ones who are paying your bills so it is not a bad idea to treat them with a little respect. You will be able to make sure that you are getting the best results possible with the options that you have when you are nice to your tenants. Respect is a two-way street so you should always do your part.

Offer Incentives

The biggest incentive is that, if they pay their rent, they will get to continue living in the house that you own. That should be enough for some people but, for others, it is not. You need to make some incentives for paying rent on time and making sure that your tenants are going to be able to enjoy the things that you have to offer them. Consider all of the various options. For example, for every 10 months that they pay on time, give them half off of their next month's rent. The chance is that this is the cost of your expenses so you will simply not profit during that time.

You can also write this off as a tax break for yourself. It is something that is causing you to lose income so you should not have to pay taxes on it. Doing this will give you a great chance at being able to do different things with your rent. Your tenants will really feel like they are getting a deal but you don't have to let them know that you are only doing it because you want them to continue renting from you. They think that they are winning but really you both are winning in the end.

Provide a Nice Home

You don't have to have the nicest home on the block or even something that costs a lot of money but you should have a decent home that is not damaged and that does not have major problems with it when you are renting it out to people who need the home to be able to live in. There are many ways in which you can make a nice home for your tenants so be sure that you are doing everything that you can to make it as nice as possible. You may want to try different things that will allow you the chance to make the home nice so always do your best to fix it up.

This is an especially important tip when you are first getting started with the home that you have. A home that is not nice will not be easy for you to rent – even with a really low rental amount. Try to figure out the easiest and least expensive way to make the home a nice place to live. You don't have to have the newest upgrades or the most expensive finishes but you would be surprised how far a can of paint can go to make the home as nice as possible.

Give Them Breaks

You probably don't want to be cutting slack to bad tenants when they are late with rent every single month but you can do some things that will help good tenants with a break every once in a while. Doing small things for tenants go a long way and you will be surprised that they actually look at you as more of an authority figure when you do things that are compassionate.

One example would be that if your tenant comes to you and lets you know that they are having a hard time paying their rent that month because of an extenuating circumstance. Instead of charging them the late fee after they are more than a week late with the rental amount, simply waive it because you know that they are going through a hard time. Good tenants will not take advantage of you when you do that so make sure that you know that before you try and figure out the way that they are going to be doing things. It will make things work out much easier for you.

Do Not Raise Rent

There is no need to raise the rent. Your mortgage is going to be the same no matter what. This goes for cases where there is, obviously, not a lot of inflation happening. You should make sure that you are trying to do your best and that you are not going to make your tenants pay for no reason at all. This is a big chore and something that you will need to figure out on your own. It is also something that you need to make happen for your tenants. If you don't raise the rent, the tenants will have more trust in you. They will be more likely to pay the rent that is owed to you and they will be more likely to continue being your tenant for years to come.

If you simply keep the rent amount around the same, it will make things easier for your tenants. It will also make it easier for you to be able to keep the tenants and to have them last for a long time. Since there is no real need for you to raise rent then you won't have to worry about the problems that come along with doing so.

Mistakes that Property Managers Make

It is not uncommon for property managers to make mistakes when they are handling the property that they have. There are major mistakes that you can make both when you are first getting a property that you can invest in and rent out as well as mistakes that you can make when you are actually renting it out. While these mistakes are relatively common for people to make, it is something that you must make sure that you are prepared for. Knowing the mistakes and what they are will make it easier for you to avoid the mistakes when you are in different situations.

Not Studying Up on Homes

Unless you look around and discover every one of the various options that exist to you if you are hiring properties out or finding properties to buy, the probabilities are that you'll more often than not find something for an improved price when that you close on the one that you've chosen. Because of this, you should check around and make an effort to figure out what will do the job and what there may be to compare to the house that you will be considering purchasing - just ensure that it is possible to figure out what's worthwhile and what's not.

No Research on the Homes Around You

Before you check around, you'll need to do research about your neighborhood. Whether this simply means that you look at different properties or get into depth about the many rental locally, the study will be good for you. You may realize that you can get a far greater price over a home (and an increased local rental margin) that is comparable but only 30 kilometers away. The study that you do will more often than not pay off over time so as to ensure that you're getting just what you want from it.

Jumping in Without Caution

If you make an effort to decide on what you are doing prematurely and you do not know the proper way to have the ability to handle the local rental process or unless you do enough research or build-up to what you do, you won't get what you will want from the rental property. It's important to make certain that you invest some time. Although it can be really enjoyable to begin with, don't take action too early or you will repent it rather than have the ability to make the money that you would like.

Not Putting Up the Cash

If you are buying property, you'll need some capital to begin with. Whether your capital is for the deposit or you have kept up even more than that for renovations and changes to your options to have, you'll be able to truly have an easier time if you just build-up a whole lot of capital. There are various options as it pertains to your rentals process so make certain as the money that is required to have the ability to afford it.

Charging Up for the Value

Don't make an effort to replace a higher price by charging too much for the local rental. You will need to make certain that your rentals are consistent with what you are really doing. Additionally, it is smart to try to make the rentals as nice as is feasible. Even though you are providing it as an "as is" local rental, you still want something nice that folks can purchase from you. There are so many choices for renovating your rental you don't even need to invest plenty of money to make it as nice as possible.

Not Fitting in with Other Options

This moves along challenging other choices that are incorporated with your rental. You do not want the purchase price to be high. No matter whether your home loan is high (and, if it's, you almost certainly shouldn't have committed to the first place). Factors to consider that you will be pricing consistent with what's common locally and that you will be not looking to get greedy with your options that are contained in your investment. There are various things that can be done but just don't make it too much for folks to afford.

Not Showing People the Right Interest

Are you truly considering the right kind of tenants? When you have a dilapidated home that you purchased from a public sale coming in at 600 dollars per month, you probably shouldn't be targeting young specialists who are making 100,000 + us dollars per yr. Instead, you should be targeting folks who are lower income. They are the ones who will be interested at home and you will be more inclined to lease it out. Together with the economy, just how that it's, you ought to have no trouble hiring out a home. If you're having trouble, for the reason that you aren't properly targeting.

Focusing on the Tenants Instead of their Background

Always check the backdrop and credit of tenants. This will protect you. Take a look at their rental record and even get personal references from them so you will have the ability to determine why they are really no more living where they did before. You don't need to require tenants to truly have a perfect 800 credit history but if indeed they have a wide array of unpaid commitments, it could be really risky that you try to rent to them.

Giving Up on the Goals

If you are considering rental purchases, it may seem to be overwhelming. Just scanning this book could make you rethink your own preference to invest. Don't allow it effect you though. Ensure that you are ready for rentals investment before you leave. You should attempt to discover anything that you can about the procedure before you give up so you can learn approximately you can about any of it. Unless you try to replace it, you will not have the ability to add all the options that you would like to your rentals process. You will likely regret not committing when you do.

Conclusion

Rental Property investing is a great way to make money, but it is not for everyone. After reading this book, you should be aware of whether or not rental property investing is the right option for you or if you want to invest in real estate in a different way.

Your next step is to invest time in figuring out your real estate market and the potential types of properties available to you. You may find one type of property is better suited to your needs, but also remember that you may have to search for the right location, property, and price.

There are benefits, as well as disadvantages of getting into investments in this manner. It is not a magic solution for you to find the right property the first time you go online and look.

As long as you keep your outlook for investing real, then you will succeed. The slow and steady one will win the race to a decent retirement, versus the one that rushes into investing without a proper strategy, funding method, and correct attitude in place.

You can get the second vacation home, the dream holiday, or retirement you desire. All you need to do is treat rental property investing like a business and believe in yourself. Please leave a review on the same place you purchased this book.

www.ingramcontent.com/pod-product-compliance
Lightning Source LLC
Chambersburg PA
CBHW070439180526
45158CB00019B/1769